D0232821

beatitude

beatitude

Relearning Jesus through Truth, Contradiction, and a Folded Dollar Bill

Matthew Paul Turner

Revell
Grand Rapids, Michigan

© 2006 by Matthew Paul Turner

Published by Fleming H. Revell
a division of Baker Publishing Group
P.O. Box 6287, Grand Rapids, MI 49516-6287
www.revellbooks.com

Printed in the United States of America

All rights reserved. No part of this publication may be reproduced, stored in a retrieval system, or transmitted in any form or by any means—for example, electronic, photocopy, recording—without the prior written permission of the publisher. The only exception is brief quotations in printed reviews.

Library of Congress Cataloging-in-Publication Data
Turner, Matthew Paul, 1973–
    Beatitude : relearning Jesus through truth, contradiction, and a folded dollar bill / Matthew Paul Turner.
      p. cm.
    ISBN 10: 0-8007-3093-3 (pbk.)
    ISBN 978-0-8007-3093-2 (pbk.)
    1. Bible. N.T. Matthew V—Criticism, interpretation, etc. 2. Beatitudes—Criticism, interpretation, etc. I. Title.
BS2575.52.T87 2006
226.9'306—dc22   2006017763

Unless otherwise indicated, Scripture is taken from the *Holy Bible*, New Living Translation, copyright © 1996. Used by permission of Tyndale House Publishers, Inc., Wheaton, Illinois 60189. All rights reserved.

Scripture marked The Message is taken from *The Message* by Eugene H. Peterson, copyright © 1993, 1994, 1995, 2000, 2001, 2002. Used by permission of NavPress Publishing Group. All rights reserved.

Scripture marked NIV is taken from the HOLY BIBLE, NEW INTERNATIONAL VERSION®. NIV®. Copyright © 1973, 1978, 1984 by International Bible Society. Used by permission of Zondervan. All rights reserved.

DISCLAIMER: In some cases, names, places, and events in this book have been altered or condensed for narrative flow. These changes do not diminish the essential integrity of the context and message of the original stories.

for jessica,
thank you for the magic you bring into my life. you are loved.

contents

the meaning of magic

It was day two at Creation, a large sweaty Christian music festival in Pennsylvania. Thousands of people come from all over the United States to attend Creation. I had only attended once before. This time, I was volunteering—artist security. That made me laugh. My then 135-pound frame probably didn't make too many artists feel all that secure. But to be honest, the volunteer position made me feel a little important; I had access to the places most commoners couldn't go. Sadly, I still had to use the bathrooms with everybody else.

I wasn't in the happiest of moods that day. I'm never too happy when I'm forced to stand in long lines for a Porta Potty. Whenever I'm at a festival, I usually try to avoid having to go to the bathroom. If I'm lucky, a mild case of constipation will ensue, which can certainly be a mood killer. But I would much rather feel constipated than sit down on a spot where thousands of people have already sat and dispersed of their bodily waste. Sometimes you just have to go. So, as I was leaving the grossest Porta-Potty experience of my entire life thus far, I heard a loud voice yelling for someone. I looked. The man was yelling at me.

"Are you yelling for me?" I asked. I didn't know the tall, lanky man.

"Yeah, I'm talking to you," he said as loudly as he could without truly yelling. Although he was still very loud. So I hesitated.

"Come over here, kid," he said. "I need something from you."

The man's glance was harsh, like I had done something wrong. Back then I didn't usually talk to strangers. I know that seems silly, but my mom had taught me to fear strangers. "You never know when someone is going to try and hurt you," she'd say to me. "So, always use common sense." I did have a bad feeling about this guy, and I thought about walking away. But for some reason, whether because he was an older man and I figured I could outrun him or the fact I was no longer a child, I walked toward him.

"Give me a dollar," said the man.

The first thing I noticed about the stranger was that he spoke very quickly; kind of like I imagined a vacuum salesman would have talked if I had lived in the fifties, when vacuum salesmen were popular. The second thing I noticed was that he was wearing flannel and corduroy in ninety-plus-degree humid heat. *This guy's a freak*, I thought

He had to be the most obnoxious needy person I had ever come in contact with. Why couldn't he just sit on a roadside with a sign that read "Need Money" like other vagabonds I had seen? And if he was so poor, how did he pay for his admission into the festival? I was skeptical.

"Why do you need a dollar?" I asked. "What are you going to do with it?" I stared at the stranger; I looked him up and down, waiting for him to offer an answer that would make me feel comfortable about handing him money. "Hey, wait a minute," I added. "You're not going to buy drugs with this money, are you?"

"*No!*" he said. "Are you kidding me, kid? Do you think your measly dollar would buy me anything worth smoking at a *Christian* music festival?"

He laughed out loud at his own funny. I only smiled.

"Come on, just give me a dollar."

Still feeling perplexed by the stranger, I begrudgingly reached into my pocket and slowly searched among the lint, old receipts, and money. I was certain I had a dollar bill I could give him. When I had found one of my scrunched-up dollars, I pulled it out, and against my good, conservative judgment, I handed it to the stranger.

"Well, I'll see you later," I said, just wanting to get away from this man. "I need to get back to my job."

"Wait! Don't go anywhere," he said; his voice was raspy, like it had to work to get up and out of his throat. "I ain't finished with you quite yet."

His comment startled me. *Am I in danger?* But despite feeling a bit freaked out, I turned around. "What do you want now, sir?"

"Watch this, young man!"

"Watch what?" I asked. The stranger didn't answer me.

Instead, he took my one-dollar bill and began to slowly smooth it out with his large, soft-looking hands. The way his hands moved, so delicately and intentionally, somewhat hypnotized me. And the sound—the sound was making my ears tickle. There's something about the sound of money crinkling between fingers that delights my senses. I suddenly felt drawn to watch him.

After he had smoothed all of the wrinkles out of the dollar bill, he held it loosely in his hands. He showed me the picture of George Washington and smiled. Then he held the dollar bill faceup and stretched out tight between his two hands. He then slowly and gently folded it over so the big number ones at the top of the bill were kissing the smaller ones at the bottom. Once he had the bill perfectly folded, he ran two fingers along the folded end and created the perfect crease. Then he folded it so that the words ONE DOLLAR printed at the bottom backside of the bill were cut in half. The stranger folded the bill again, and again. He folded it once more and then he stopped. I don't believe he could have folded it another time.

He then raised his head, looked at me, and then looked at the small folded bill in his large hand. As he stared purposefully at me, his hands began moving again. My eyes had trouble making up their mind; they kept moving from the man's eyes to his hands and back again. He unfolded the dollar bill one fold at a time, slowly, with intent. Each movement of his hands made the bill larger. When he finally unfolded the last bend in the bill and smoothed it out perfectly with his fingers, I could not believe what my eyes were seeing.

"I believe this bill is yours, my young friend," said the stranger. And then the man handed me a brand-new, twenty-dollar bill. He smiled the biggest grin I have ever seen. It wasn't a pretty grin; his teeth were stained and not too straight, but it was still a comforting smile.

"How on earth did you do that?" I asked, my demeanor having changed from skepticism to awe.

Ignoring my question, the stranger started walking away. I yelled again.

"Hey, wait a minute; how did you do that?"

He didn't look back; he didn't even flinch at the sound of my voice; he just kept walking.

"How did you do that?" I yelled as loudly as I could, my voice

gaining the attention of many other festival attendees standing close by.

The stranger didn't stop walking. But he did finally reply. "My name is George, and what you just witnessed, my friend, was magic. Now, you know I can't tell you the secret of my magic." George laughed a big hearty laugh. "But the twenty-dollar bill is yours! Keep it! I've got more than enough of those."

I watched George walk away and eventually disappear into the crowd.

Shocked, embarrassed, and humbled, I folded the twenty-dollar bill a couple times and shoved it into my pocket.

I think about George and his magic trick a lot. I could have watched him do that trick over and over again and still never have seen his hands switch out my one-dollar bill with the brand-new twenty that he had hidden somewhere up his sleeve or in his pocket. No *real* magic was there that day—I know that. It was simply a case of his hand being quicker than my eye. But knowing that didn't make the experience any less magical for me.

Magical is not about the silly trick, at least, it wasn't for me. The magical is what happens when the hand has finished being quicker than the eye. Magical is the grin left on the face of the small kid when an ordinary father pretends to pull a penny out of an ear. Magical is the gasp of excitement from a crowd when a magician has seemingly sawed a person in half. Changing a one-dollar bill into a twenty was certainly a fun little magic trick that George had mastered, but it wasn't magical.

The amazement and disbelief and even embarrassment that was left on my face and tingling through my senses when George handed me the twenty—that was magical. To George, it was simply a trick, something he probably did all of the time; it was obviously something he enjoyed doing. But for me, George's silly little trick was much more.

That peculiar little meeting with George has toyed with my brain for more than ten years. Strangely enough, it's made me ponder my own life from time to time. As I have retold that story many times, I've had to wonder if anyone has ever considered me to be the least bit magical. Do I leave behind any kind of an impression?

I've often asked myself what kind of emotion and feeling I leave on the minds and hearts of people when I am finished talking. How do my attitudes and opinions affect a roomful of people? Does my spirit emote peace in a roomful of strangers? When people walk away from an interaction with me, are they ever left amazed? In other words, do the people I come in contact with see even a hint of Jesus in my life? Do they experience anything remotely pure, humbling, true—magical?

Back in early 2000, I watched songwriter Nichole Nordeman introduce a roomful of stuffy music business executives to her song "Every Season." Before that day, I had been to numerous events like this. They'd pretty much all been the same. The mood of the room is usually polite at best. Men and women are dressed in their best blue and black suits accented with only a touch of color. Anything too extravagant would be considered flashy and uncool.

I don't believe you're allowed to attend an event like this without having the look of annoyance written all over your face. It's an expression which hangs somewhere between taking oneself too seriously and experiencing utter distress. It's considered cool at these events if you can give off the vibe that you have a million places where you could (and would rather) be. These people aren't impressed with showcases. They have seen hundreds of artists parade themselves and their talents across this type of stage many times before. They're not rude, well, most of them aren't rude. It's not like they resist applauding, but they don't go out of their way. They aren't there doing everything they can to make an artist feel at home.

But on that particular day, as Nichole shared her story behind the song, something was very different about the way the crowd responded—people began to listen. As she began to play the simple piano melody over the last few moments of her story, I watched as a thousand businesspeople got quiet and reflective. No one talked. The service people stopped serving. People put down their drinks. They stopped eating their desserts. Having not witnessed anything like this at a music business function, I couldn't help but soak it up. For four and a half minutes, Nichole's song had the complete attention of a roomful of seemingly unmovable, uppity business-types.

When she finished singing and the last note on the piano was played, the applause from the crowd was thunderous and alive—most of them stood up. I had chills, not because of the song (I had heard it before), but because I had just witnessed something beautiful happen. The room was thick with it. Nichole's grace and words and message did something in the room I rarely have witnessed before at an event like this. As Nichole stood up from the piano and walked offstage, I watched as people leaned over to each other and shook their heads in amazement. I watched people—professional people—wipe away tears from their eyes. Something in the room that day was unexplainable, and I observed it moving the hearts of some pretty hard-to-crack people.

I sat in the back of the room, a bit dazzled in disbelief.

Something about that moment was magical.

Henry Blackaby's book *Experiencing God* influenced me to get involved with the will of God and not the will of myself. His thoughts on hearing God's voice intrigued me enough to explore the presence of God myself. Several years ago, I got the chance to interview Dr. Blackaby. The thought of interviewing one of my influences intimidated me a little. And I had reason to be intimidated: He was old; I was very young. He was wise; I was probably quite foolish. He was educated and astute; at the time, I was an untrained writer in *way* over my head.

When the day came to meet him face-to-face, I was a wreck. Every place on my body that had sweat glands was working overtime. I had to keep my arms down and by my side because I could tell the pits of my shirt were stained with sweat. Eventually, Dr. Blackaby's warm and friendly personality put my nervousness at ease. I found him to be kind of grandfatherly, in a good way. Dressed in a blue three-piece suit, this Santa-like individual talked with me for more than an hour like I was the only person he cared about.

I fell in love with his stories.

The old man talked about his wife as though the two had just fallen in love yesterday. He spoke of his kids as if they were the very reason he was alive. But when he talked about Jesus, that was when he felt most at home. Or at least, it seemed that way. Up until that day, I don't believe I had ever heard anyone speak about a friendship with Jesus like him. One might describe him as passionate, but I don't believe *passion* even begins to explain it, really. I *felt* something when I was with that old gentle soul. It was as though Jesus was sitting at the table with us, but he was *his* friend, not mine. I know that sounds strange, and I can't perfectly describe what it felt like, but I believe Jesus was there. And he wanted to be there.

As I listened to the stories, I felt like I was sitting down and having a cup of coffee with Moses. The sarcastic side of me wanted to take Dr. Blackaby to a large body of water to see if he could do anything cool and miraculous to it. Even if he couldn't make it stand up like two great walls, I wouldn't have been too surprised if he would have been able to do something with it. Unfortunately, we were in Atlanta.

Whether or not he could have made water stand up tall was probably a very stupid thought, but it was clear to me Dr. Blackaby had spent a great deal of time getting to know Jesus. His relationship with Jesus had aged like a good cabernet. As I sat there, listening to him talk about intimacy with an unseen being, I couldn't help but feel my own spirituality was trite and unfinished. It seemed to me Jesus and Dr. Blackaby were the best of friends.

Thinking all these things got me wondering how Jesus sees his relationship with me. Being that I was, at the time, quite insecure, I became thoroughly convinced he must look at my relationship with him and feel like a distant relative or an ex-lover.

Meeting Dr. Blackaby made me feel amazement, disbelief, and embarrassment, exactly the same feelings I experienced when George turned my dollar bill into a twenty. Sure, the two experiences are very different, but both left me feeling similar emotions. When I got up from the table, I shook his hand, knowing this wasn't just an interview.

Dr. Blackaby left me wanting some of what he had. I walked away desiring to believe more deeply in the things of Jesus. I walked away thirstier and hungrier.

Something about my meeting with Dr. Blackaby was magical. Much like other encounters, I can't explain it.

But I'm learning I don't necessarily have to.

Anytime Jesus walks with a person on their journey, I expect to be amazed. The experiences of my past that evoke an honest, true, and miraculous response stay with me. The emotions those experiences make me feel and the lessons they teach me almost always get written into my God-story, the thread of life you know isn't accidental.

When I encounter the "magic," I do my best to make those stories become a part of who I am as I strive to walk with Jesus in this life. These experiences teach me more about who he is. And because of the God-things I encounter, sometimes I become a little more like he asks me to be. It's in these moments that the truth of the Gospel becomes more alive in my life. But I don't want it to simply come alive; I want the effects of that message to change me. I want those changes to affect how I live. I believe Jesus wants the way I live to leave people, the ones he has put in my path, feeling like they just witnessed somebody turn a one-dollar bill into a twenty.

Some might think this type of thinking is lofty.

A few might call it controversial.

Isn't it true that Jesus wants our lives to invoke a sense of spiritual wonder in the people we meet, in the things we do? That's what I desire.

But gosh, it's a struggle to live like that. Big parts of my "Christian" life, with all of its pain, mistakes, bad information, conflicts with mean-spirited Christians, and *being* mean-spirited myself at times, had so misshaped me that I was lost, nowhere close to knowing Jesus. Well, I knew a version of Jesus, just not his.

A new education became necessary.

I wasn't on a journey. I was standing still in what I considered to be the perfect Jesus-spot.

The book you're holding is a collection of stories, conversations, and thoughts about becoming weak enough to step out of my comfort zone and to begin walking with Jesus on a journey—a journey toward relearning everything about him. It still seems a little funny to say that out loud—*relearning Jesus*. But that's exactly what is happening in my life. Through the stories I am about to share, I learned that embracing faith in Jesus is not only something full of mystery and truth, but it is also a journey constantly moving, growing, listening, falling down, wrestling, experiencing, and humbling.

And once in a while, it's revealing.

Something very powerful is found in the most simple expressions of Jesus. The effects of his words in Matthew 5—the Beatitudes—have been a very influential part of my life. Sure, they're simplistic; sometimes so much so that I've skipped over them or thought I knew them or forgotten them.

And I have ignored them.

These teachings befuddle me. Sometimes I feel lost and empty because of the way these words convict. Sometimes they make only a little sense, but perhaps that's because they're hard. Every once in a while I actually get quiet and humble enough to let the Beatitudes affect how I live my life. Isn't that sad? I've been following Jesus since I was four and only a few years ago did I get weak enough to take another look at who Jesus is in light of the things he said in Matthew 5. That's what these stories are about. My relearning of Jesus through the "lens" of Matthew 5.

Thirteen years ago, Jesus pulled me off of that "spot" and asked me to begin journeying with him. The experience was quite burdensome at first. But despite the questions I had in my head, I decided to just begin. Little did I know, Jesus wanted me to meet him again, not like I had when I was a child, or the way I experienced him as a teenager, but meet him as if it were the very first time. This book chronicles my journey, or at least the parts of the journey worthy of retelling. These stories and thoughts continue to be awakenings in my life as I learn (or relearn) what it means to walk with Jesus on this journey, and to be like him to those who travel on the road with me.

And of course, as you read about the people, places, and events that have dotted my road, I hope it helps you begin to see your own spiritual life as a journey and not a destination.

Thank you for walking with me.

Matthew Paul Turner

a short word before

On the day I read Matthew 5 for what had to be at least the *thousandth* time, I was drinking something that certainly resembled coffee, but it wasn't coffee. By the time it had been blended together with ice, chocolate, caramel, and heavy cream and then topped with something white, whipped, and sweet, the flavor of my Thailand coffee was completely masked. Despite all of that, the drink tasted good. And was helping me stay awake.

The little coffeehouse was quite warm, even though it was only a few degrees higher than forty outside. I thought about taking my Duke University sweatshirt off, but I was feeling lazy, so I didn't.

I'm sure I appeared very evangelical to all who might have noticed me sitting alone. My big green Bible was wide open and placed perfectly out on the round table in front of me. I had it open to Matthew 5 because I desperately needed to hear Jesus talk. My personal bout with pornography (a story I share in *Provocative Faith*) had seemingly caused Jesus to not talk to me. It had been five days since our last conversation, and I'm not sure he had ever gone that long without talking to me before.

a short word before

A word of advice from one of my friends was that I should read
Matthew 5. I had read Matthew 5 many times. It had always been
a passage I liked, but by that time in my life, every time I reread
it, it just seemed like words on a page. But that day's reading of
Matthew 5 was different. These are the words I read.

One day as the crowds were gathering, Jesus went up the mountainside with his disciples and sat down to teach them. This is
what he taught them:

"God blesses those who realize their need for him,
    for the Kingdom of Heaven is given to them.
God blesses those who mourn,
    for they will be comforted.
God blesses those who are gentle and lowly,
    for the whole earth will belong to them.
God blesses those who are hungry and thirsty for justice,
    for they will receive it in full.
God blesses those who are merciful,
    for they will be shown mercy.
God blesses those whose hearts are pure,
    for they will see God.
God blesses those who work for peace,
    for they will be called the children of God.
God blesses those who are persecuted because they live for
    God,
    for the Kingdom of Heaven is theirs.

"God blesses you when you are mocked and persecuted and lied
about because you are my followers. Be happy about it! Be very
glad! For a great reward awaits you in heaven. And remember, the
ancient prophets were persecuted, too.

"You are the salt of the earth. But what good is salt if it has lost its flavor? Can you make it useful again? It will be thrown out and trampled underfoot as worthless. You are the light of the world—like a city on a mountain, glowing in the night for all to see. Don't hide your light under a basket! Instead, put it on a stand and let it shine for all. In the same way, let your good deeds shine out for all to see, so that everyone will praise your heavenly Father."

Matthew 5:1–16

As soon as I finished reading, I closed my Bible. Instead of looking around, I put my forehead down against my Bible's faux leather cover. I sat there with my eyes closed and my head against the face of my Bible for thirty minutes. I'm not sure what people thought of me. I'm sure I looked ridiculous, but I didn't care.

For those minutes, I said nothing. I thought about nothing. I did nothing. I just remained quiet and still. Music played over the speakers, but I couldn't tell you what songs. I'm sure people came and sat down near me, but I didn't know it. I remained still, numbed by what I read.

I walked into that coffeehouse that day expecting Jesus to talk, and I figured if he were going to speak, I wanted to be quiet.

When I came out of my little God "trance," Jesus made one thing clear. It wasn't much. He didn't sit down and have a conversation with me like I thought he might; he just put this verse on my heart: "God blesses those whose hearts are pure, for they will see God."

I wanted to see God. In fact, I was desperately needing to see God.

I stood up quickly to leave the coffeehouse. When I picked up my Bible, the corner of it hit my cold chocolate coffee drink. I watched its contents spill and splatter all over everything that was anywhere near me. Everywhere I looked I saw a brownish milky substance with chunks of deflated whipped cream in it. The frothy mixture spilled all over the nicely painted floor, the expensive chairs, the table with a checkerboard painted in the middle, and to my horror, on one of the other customers.

"Oh sir, I am *so sorry!*" I said with as much meaning and feeling as I could put into a short, quick sentence.

The gentleman, who was dressed in a sport coat and a pair of seventies-looking dress pants, stood up as fast as he could to miss the rest of the drink pouring down from the side of the table.

"Oh, *crap!*" I said. "I am *so* sorry."

"Don't worry about it, boy," said the man rather nicely. "Honestly, I am just glad to know that you are alive."

We were both on our hands and knees cleaning up the mess with small napkins.

"What?"

"I'm not kidding; you sat there with your head against your Bible for so long that I was very close to shaking you or calling 9-1-1. I didn't know what to think."

"Oh, I was just being still. I am sorry that I got coffee all over you."

"It's *OK*."

It took me nearly fifteen minutes to get all of the coffee wiped up.

"Well, sir, I am leaving; thank you so much for helping me clean up the mess."

"Oh, no problem. I'm used to helping clean up messes. My dad always said, 'Cleanliness is next to godliness.'"

The man paused for a moment, as if he were thinking, *I sound like my father!*

"I always hated that stupid little saying."

"Why?" I asked.

"Because it doesn't mention one d—— thing about all of the

hard work and all the s—— you have to go through to get things clean."

He laughed.

I walked out of the coffeehouse fast, like I was on a mission. The kind man's words made me realize I had a lot of cleaning up to do.

Truthfully, every time I read Jesus's words in Matthew 5, I realize how much cleaning up I need to do.

1

peace

Nonviolence means avoiding not only external physical violence but also internal violence of spirit. You not only refuse to shoot a man, but you refuse to hate him.

Martin Luther King Jr.

I'm often bewildered by the words of Jesus. Blessed are the peacemakers?! What was he thinking? I've learned over the years that peacemaking is hard work. In fact, at times I wonder if it's even possible. I sometimes wonder why Jesus couldn't have made it easier for us humans. Why couldn't he have said, "Blessed are the selfish"? I could have easily fallen in line with that. Being selfish, in most instances, is much simpler than peacemaking.

But Jesus didn't make it easy. In fact, few of Jesus's words seem easy. But when he said, "Blessed are the peacemakers," he raised his expectation for humanity. And sometimes I think he set the bar too high.

Nonetheless, Jesus longed for the people of his time to live their lives with peace in mind. And not just any kind of peace—his kind of peace.

That's a very different way of life than what they had been used to living.

When Jesus first spoke those words, I can only imagine how many blank and awkward stares he got from the crowd. Sure, some people sitting on the mountainside were probably awestruck and humbled by his words. Perhaps, even most of them. But I can't help but believe a few sitting there didn't know what to think about Jesus at first. There had to be some people who were wondering, "What the h—— is this guy talking about?" I'm sure others said, "Ah, fiddlesticks! This guy's a good speaker, but he's saying all kinds of things that go against the teaching of Moses and Elijah." Still another, "This man's nothing but a bloody liar." Of course, I imagine the last guy with a British accent. For some reason, British accents make almost any phrase feel more biblical.

Of course, I can't be certain hecklers and skeptics were at the Sermon on the Mount. But sometimes I'm a heckler. And, too, look at how the messages of Jesus rub people the wrong way today; I can only imagine they must have done the same back then—even at the beginning of his ministry.

One thing I do know is that every time I think about—*really* think about—his call for me to be a peacemaker, I get annoyed, I get angry, I get frustrated with Jesus. I get this way because no matter what I am doing—good or bad—those words of Jesus—actively pursue making peace—scrape up against my nature. They are like salt against my overbitten fingernails.

I think peacemaking is some of the hardest kind of living.

peace

It's more often than not the difficult way to live.

I do sometimes wish Jesus had said, "Blessed are the selfish." I think I'd be good at it.

The Peace Sign

A good friend of mine has been an activist against the war in Iraq since it began in 2003. Long before hating the war was popular, my friend stood proudly in the minority. She believed that peace needed a chance. And honestly, it's hard to argue with someone who has her kind of passion. She demonstrates it beautifully by simply believing wholeheartedly in her cause. My friend loves the idea of peace more than most of the Christians I know.

But in my opinion, she and her peace friends go a little overboard once in a while.

My friend and I came to a mutual understanding long ago: When we don't agree on politics, pop culture, and the like, our social differences won't disrupt our love for each other as friends.

Despite the work it takes to sometimes be friends, I have a lot of respect for the uphill struggle my friend pursues on behalf of "peace." She goes to meetings about peace, makes phones calls to voters about peace, and attends rallies to support peace.

I love when she goes to rallies. I look forward to her going to rallies, not because of her passionate stance and what she might accomplish but because every time she attends one of her rallies, she always returns with hilarious, nonpeaceful stories about certain participants.

On one occasion she returned from a rally with a story about one of the guys from her "peace club" throwing a bucket of paint at a police officer. He, of course, was arrested. Another time, while marching in a nearby city, she and a friend of hers led the entire parade down the wrong street. Her peace friends were *furious*. In fact, a few of them got so mad they left the rally right then and there. But my favorite story was the time she tripped and fell down right in front of a White House guard at the largest of all anti-war demonstrations (well, for the Iraq war anyway). The guard, a large African-American man dressed in uniform, actually helped her up off the ground while the rest of her group continued their march. My friend eventually caught up with the others, but it was too late; they had already passed the spot where they got as close to the White House as the authorities would let them, and to her frustration, she missed out on meeting Martin Sheen.

Every war demonstration she attends brings a new story.

"Oh, I was so disgusted today, Matthew," she said to me a couple of years ago. I wish you could see her. When my friend tells stories, it's important that you're in the same room. She's very expressive. Her hands move up and down. Her face gets red. And sometimes she curses in Italian. Oh, and she talks very fast when she gets hyperpassionate. And on this particular day, her emotion and passion were out in full force.

"You *will* not believe this, Matthew," she said. "There we were trying to have a peace rally, a *peace* rally, mind you, when all of a sudden about fifty people from who the heck knows where begin forcing their way through the police line. It was awful. I got sprayed with some kind of police gas; lucky for me I had my back turned, so it hit *and stained* my jacket. And I wasn't even doing anything wrong. It was all of these other people rushing the line. I was trying to spread peace, and they were making a ruckus. I'm almost positive it was a bunch of right-wingers trying to make our peace rally go sour. It had to be . . . and of course, the news cameras only cover the *crazies*. Oh, it turned into a *huge* mess."

"That sounds *very* peaceful," I said. "I'm really sorry I missed that."

30

She just glared at me.

"Well, did anyone read your sign?" I asked, trying to change the subject before she could. She had taken a great deal of time to create this rather cleverly designed sign that read, "GIVE US PEACE, IN THE MIDDLE EAST, HELP US STOP THE BEAST!" Believe me, I wish you could have seen the sign; the design was much more impressive than the slogan. The slogan was pretty dreadful, but I didn't have the heart to tell her.

"Yes, a few people read it; I think a *Washington Post* photographer took a picture of me holding it. So, maybe I'll get close to the dream of what every peace activist longs for: I'll be on the front page tomorrow morning," she said, mocking herself. My friend then looked at me like something was terribly wrong. "Can I ask you a question?"

"Sure."

"Do you think I'm crazy for doing this kind of stuff?"

"No. Why would you think that?"

"Are you sure?"

"I don't think you're crazy. You're doing something you believe in, and I respect that. Now, I don't always think something 'peaceful' comes out of those kinds of things. I'm just not sure you can *rally* for peace. That's all."

"I know. Today was just awful."

"Do you think you helped the cause for peace today?" I asked.

"I know I'm not sounding very 'Democrat' by saying this, but I don't think we did," she said with a serious smirk. "I don't think one person was influenced by what we did today. Not one."

"But aren't you missing the point?" I asked. "Isn't the point of a peace rally to simply let the government know that you disagree with the way they are handling things?"

"I honestly don't know what the point is; I've just always done it—ever since I was in college," she said laughing. "President Bush wasn't even at the White House today. So he didn't hear us."

"I'm sure Karl Rove will give him the message," I replied.

She stuck her finger in her mouth and pretended to gag.

"Let me ask you a question," I said. "Do you think Jesus would *ever* be at a peace rally?"

"I don't know. I think if he were to come to one, he'd have something to say about how we actually do it. Do you think he could find a way to make twenty thousand people be peaceful? I'm telling you, it's hard work; especially when we're all screaming, 'We want peace! We want peace!'"

"I'm sure he'd never go," I said.

"Why not?"

"It just doesn't seem to be his kind of peace."

"I think it is," she said with confidence. "So do you think I'll be on the cover of the *Washington Post* tomorrow morning?"

"Maybe. It would be kind of fun."

"I know; I'm gonna go call Mom."

She wasn't on the front page of the paper; Bush was. The rally got a mention on page 12A.

Thoughts on War and Peace

I have had many conversations with that friend (and other friends too) about the protesting of war and how it relates to the peace Jesus asks us to make. But as much as my friends think they're fighting the good fight of faith when they protest, I'm pretty sure the peace that gets yelled for and turned into clever slogans at peace rallies is *not* the same kind of peace Jesus talks about.

When I lived in the Washington DC area, I saw several peace rallies. Watching them over the years, I became convinced that the peace demanded during those wartime gatherings is a one-dimensional type of peace. In other words, in nearly every case I witnessed, protestors were just looking for the kind of peace that gets one side (or both) to drop their weapons and retreat or not go to war at all.

But that isn't necessarily peace; at least, it's not the type of peace Jesus described. The type of peacemaking Jesus refers to in the Beatitudes is not about simply giving up; it's not about dropping weapons and returning home.

Brother Andrew addresses peace in his book *Light Force*. He writes that true peace is not possible anywhere, in any situation, under any circumstances, without Jesus. It's impossible.

Can I be honest? I don't get all that excited when I think about peace not being possible without Jesus. Like any normal human being, I want the Iraq war to be over. I want Israel and Palestine to get along. I want Democrats and Republicans to work together for the good of our country. However, I also know what it takes for there to be peace between my wife and me. And if it's a problem at that level, peace is hard to come by.

Brother Andrew thinks that is why Jesus is called the Prince of Peace. If he's the *Prince* of all things peaceful, surely he is needed in a situation for peace to even be an option.

In most cases, we humans really haven't a clue what peace is like. We have an idea—an idea that gets presented to us by historians, the media, and others. I've learned if I want to have any chance at being a maker of peace in the world around me and in my personal life, I have to *know* peace when I see it.

Before my journey began, I only knew when I didn't see it.

A Bigger Lesson about Peace*making*

When Jesus walked on this earth, he was obviously the greatest of peacemakers. He achieved a popular following because he made peace by calming seas, casting out demons, and healing broken and sinful hearts. When he calmed people's situations, it wasn't simply an end to their painful circumstances; he didn't just help them out of their problems. He made them whole again. Those people who Jesus impacted experienced a fullness they had never begun to imagine was possible. That's what the peace of Jesus is about—filling up the taker and making them whole.

It's certainly easy for Jesus to do such things. He had only to walk into a situation and peace would occur if he deemed it appropriate. He didn't have to speak anything, or do anything miraculous; many times his presence was enough to bring peace and calm to the lives he touched. His life on earth, and now through the Spirit of God, was about bringing wholeness to the lives of people.

Over the years, through many circumstances, I've learned the kind of peace Jesus mandates from us is about bringing his wholeness in our own situations.

In several places throughout Eugene Peterson's *The Message*, he uses the word *wholeness* in spots where other translations use *peace*. The word *wholeness* implies the peace we find in Jesus and the peace we *make* through Jesus is always about reconciliation. It's about a human being finding true completion.

Peacemaking is not simply about having working relations between two countries or two entities or two people. Sure, that might be a small part of what Jesus was trying to communicate, but like most of his core messages, the peacemaking he talks about has more to do with the condition of human hearts. He doesn't expect us to *just* put down our guns; we have to take many more actions for peace to be possible. He knows that out of a person's heart comes the actions and personality for non-peace. Those actions are a reflection of what's going on inside of us. It's the old "what goes up, must come down" theory, but this time it's "what's inside will eventually come out."

Throughout history world leaders have struggled to balance the relationship between war and peace. It's easy to look back over history and remember the great wars. Wars stick out in history like large black blotches on white paper. When peace is unavailable or fails to exist, the memory is long. Jesus knew that about non-peace; he knew that stench of unrest and war wreaks havoc on a society's well-being. But the struggle to make peace is not a macro problem. It almost always begins with an individual heart.

As we know all too well, peace is a struggle for humanity in general, in all levels of life—work, family, and relationships. Wherever people exist, peace is problematic. And so often, just like a glance back in history reminds us quickly of our ancestors' mistakes, when we look at our own personal history, we often see the most vivid memories are ones where peace is nowhere to be found.

This is true in my own life, at least. In fact, it has been within the confines of Christian culture I have suffered the most effects of non-peace.

Peace, Love, and Christians

I've watched Christians struggle making peace. When I was a child growing up in an unusually conservative church, peace was something like an enigma.

Church often frustrated my father. It's hard to think of a time when Dad would not come home angry from our church's deacons' meetings. Dad was one of seven men who had been voted in by the church membership to manage the direction of the church. And boy, peace struggled to exist around that circle. They'd argue over almost anything—money, politics, rules, salvation methods—it was a smorgasbord of topics.

beatitude

When I knew Dad was having a Thursday night deacons' meeting, I got anxious. Often my mom, sisters, and I would gather in a circle and pray that Dad would have wisdom and patience in those meetings. More often than not our prayers seemed to go unanswered. In seventh grade, one of my closest and dearest friends since first grade left our church's Christian school without saying good-bye to me. I thought that was a very odd thing.

Just one day, out of the blue, her name was called over the loud speaker. She was told to gather her belongings. She did, and never walked into our classroom again.

Her father had been a deacon for as long as mine had. However, a disagreement among the deacon board caused him to take action—he left the church angrily, pulled his kid from the school, and never stepped foot in the church again. I've only spoken to Alicia a couple of times since she left our school that day. The last time we chatted, it had been seven years since that event had occurred, and she was still living her life somewhat dependent on the pain she felt from our church.

It's troubling how deep pain like that can feel.

That day, I believe, was my first experience where the lack of peace within the walls of the church had very personal repercussions. It hurt to lose a friend. When Alicia left the school that day, it caused disruption among my friends and me. Kids said mean things about my father, the pastor, and the rest of the leaders. People took sides. Some left the church. Others pretended the problem didn't exist. "We need to move on," I remember many saying. And back then, I probably would have thought they were right; we did need to move on. But moving on without peace is not moving on; it's simply an existence that mentally and spiritually remains with you until you forget about it or hope is restored.

Today, when I talk to my dad about those years at the church, he shakes his head in disgust. My father, who has been a follower of Jesus for nearly forty years, has told me many times the "Lord's work" has aged him more than any other part of life. Some of his most difficult experiences in life have been when he was surrounded by Christians—Christians who couldn't get along.

Dad's not alone in this experience. I've met people of faith all over the country who would say the effort they have put into "being Christian" has brought them more pain and frustration than anything resembling peace. So many look back on their spiritual pasts and see more big black blotches of unrest than they see peace.

Is Jesus in those situations?

I think Christians should be leading the peace initiative. That's why listening to people tell me these kinds of stories leaves me feeling overwhelmed. How can we make peace in the world when we can't even make peace in our churches? Why is peace within the walls of the church hard to come by?

Many times in my life, I have been a victim of non-peace. But I've also been a perpetrator of it too. I'm guilty of being the non-peaceful man who is *inside* the church where the love of Jesus is supposed to "flow like a river." Many times I make things worse instead of more peaceful, causing the people I love alarm and worry and pain.

I believe peace dodges me because I fail to keep running back to the source of peace. Without the source, I'm a part of the problem.

Possibilities Imagined

"Matthew!"

My wife, Jessica, was yelling my name down the hallway. She

beatitude

doesn't do it too often, but when she does, I almost always know what it's about—the laundry.

Jessica is a saint for putting up with the process she has endured to de-bachelorize me. (And it's not over yet!) When it comes to doing the laundry, I can be as dumb as they come. Now, I do know the difference between whites and darks, but I don't like rules, so I occasionally put a couple of *my* white things in with the dark stuff. Maybe it's laziness, but truthfully, I don't care if my boxer-briefs have a hint of blue in them. Pink is a problem, but not blue.

However, that was *not* the problem this time around.

Usually, the "big crisis" that happens between my wife and me stems from me not cleaning out the pockets of my jeans. I've washed a lot of money, business cards, and receipts in my day. One time I left an ink pen in the dryer and got blue ink all over everything. My wife's favorite underwear had huge blue blotches on it. *She minded.* Another time, I left mustard packets from McDonald's in my shorts' pockets and put them in the washing machine. But she wasn't yelling my name for doing this, either. My lovely wife, Jessica, was yelling my name on this particular evening because I had left my wet green towel draped across the door to our bedroom. Not that big of a deal, right?

When I was single, the door was where my towel felt at home. Sure, it looked sloppy, but being a single adult for nearly twelve years had brought me a few "nonmarriable" habits. I was *young* in marriage; I was still learning. I still *am* learning. And Jessica is faithful to keep me on that journey.

"Why do you insist on putting your towel on the door?" she said, in a forceful tone. I could tell she was serious.

"Why are you making this a big deal? Why can't you just work through it?"

"*Work through it?* Why can't *you* work through it? Why can't you put your towel in the clothes hamper where it is supposed to go, or on the rack next to the shower?"

She had a point there. And I knew it. But I still wasn't willing to back down—not quite yet. I still had a few more good points in me too.

"Jessica, you're making a mountain out of a molehill. *I like the towel on the door! Do you have to change everything about my life?*"

Yeah, so that statement didn't go over too well.

My lovely wife just stared at me with a "you *did not* just go there" look on her face. Words couldn't say what we were feeling for each other at that particular moment. So, we did what comes naturally to us when we're not in the mood to make peace: we retreated to separate corners of the house. I walked about three feet into the living room and pounced down as loudly as I could on the couch. She turned around and walked two-and-a-half steps into our bedroom and slammed the door.

Except, the towel was still there.

Sometimes the simplest of situations are the hardest to make peaceful. At that point, when my wife and I were as far apart as a one-thousand-square-foot condo would allow, if peace was going to be an option, one of us was going to have to give in. One of us was going to have to admit that the other was right. Someone was going to have to get humble.

Following Jesus in this life has taught me that simply giving in and admitting the other was right would only produce a *chance* for peace. It would not promise peace. Peace required one of us to sacrifice, drop the pride, rid ourselves of the selfishness, and then make a change in our behavior. And then, *maybe*, wholeness would become a possibility.

beatitude

As I sat on my couch, alone in my living room, watching *The Apprentice*, I deliberated with God. Actually, very little deliberating was going on; he was pretty much putting me in my place. So I sat there, listening to God completely rip my "towel on the bedroom door" case to shreds. It sucks when you can't get the Savior of the world to be on your side. And from experience, I have learned nothing is ever remotely fun about being God-whipped.

Finally, after calming down from having to hear God get on my case too, I was ready to admit I was the one who could (and should) make peace possible. So, I went to my wife and apologized, and I told her that it was me who was wrong. But apologizing was only the first step; I couldn't stop there. I had to also promise that the necessary changes would be made in my lifestyle to ensure "the towel" would find a new, more suitable home.

I can't tell you how hard that was for me.

That "event" happened more than two years ago. And still, to this day, every single time I jump out of the shower and finish drying off, I still have the urge to just throw my towel over the door.

I don't do it, but gosh, it's a temptation.

Making peace, even in the small areas of life, is hard. But I believe when we're peaceful in the small things, somehow God uses those circumstances to also teach us how to make peace in the big areas of life too.

Perhaps because of my childhood church experience, I ended up having a very ill-mannered view of peacemaking. Sometimes I didn't know how to do it.

Through life, Jesus teaches me what making peace is about. He opened my eyes to the fact that I needed to learn *peace*—his kind of peace—is about making a situation whole. It's not just about ending an argument. It's not simply about taking back the mean-spirited remarks. It's about humbling oneself enough to change.

It's almost never easy to take on the attributes of Christ and present them in certain situations. But when we see it happen, it's an amazing event to witness.

A couple of years ago, I witnessed the peace of Jesus come into a very ugly situation involving a teenage girl and her youth pastor. I'm sure you can imagine the nature of the predicament, so there's no need to give much detail. Because of the sensitivity of this type of occurrence, reconciliation and peace are often not the first alternative. In most situations such as these, parents of the victim become irate, and some would likely want to *kill* the youth pastor. Many people would feel as though the family's anger would be completely justified. And sadly, church leadership often doesn't know the best way of handling this kind of situation—some want to hide it, some offer a graceless conclusion.

However, in the terrible situation I watched unfold, none of those things happened. I marveled as I witnessed a family's faith in Jesus allow them the ability to make peace not only an option in the life of this young youth pastor and their daughter; they actually walked into the situation demanding it be the *only* option. Bringing the option for peace into that kind of situation must have been excruciatingly difficult. But the pastor, along with the mother, father, and daughter, worked through a long list of necessary steps to make it possible. All of the parties who were involved met together. They talked about the situation. Tears ensued. Apologies ensued. Forgiveness and grace ensued. And ultimately, over time, wholeness ensued.

I'm not sure if I have ever witnessed anything like it. In some ways, the ability to make peace in that situation seemed almost awkward. Do I understand that kind of peacemaking exactly? Not really. But when I finally had a chance to stand back and consider the peace, I was left breathless with the love and forgiveness and peace of that mother and father.

Jesus's entire goal was to bring wholeness to the lives of people. His mission for me is to take the same wholeness he gives me and apply it to the everyday situations I experience in life.

It's hard to imagine what is possible with true peace.

Julie

I struggle with the idea of peace. I sometimes struggle making it, finding it, seeing it; peace isn't something that comes naturally to me. As with all things that Jesus teaches on the journey, I've learned that peacemaking begins with getting out of the way. People who bring peace along with them tend to be people who are pursuing lives that aren't centered on themselves. Despite knowing Jesus, or at least knowing his name, all of my life, I have grown accustomed to centering life on me. Over the years, I have realized my constant need to take care of me has prohibited my ability to be a peacemaker.

Getting out of the way is the hardest part of following Jesus. And sometimes, that's all he wants from us. He just wants us to get humble, and that's when he can use us. He's constantly having to remind me to "get out of the way, Matthew; I can't use you or the situation you're in if you're going to only focus on your needs." It's never easy when Jesus shows you a vivid picture of yourself. His words do not candy-coat the truth. That kind of humility is hard to take, but it's also needed for peace to breathe in a situation.

I've learned through experience that peacemaking is never simple. You have to be listening for Jesus's voice. I am sure I miss him more than I hear him. But once in a while I do hear him loud and clear.

Three years ago, my friend Julie was in a confusing place in life. Over the course of several months, she had lost her job, been unable to find work, and consequently was experiencing some financial struggles. Her situation had made many believe (including me) she might be battling through a bout with depression.

Julie and I have been friends since we were both three years old. Over the years, she has become more like a sister to me than a mere friend. For many years, the two of us were inseparable. When I heard from several mutual friends that Julie was having a hard time I made a point to get together with her the next time I was in my hometown.

On a late summer afternoon, while sitting in my parents' glassed-in porch, Julie began to describe what she was feeling. She explained a little about where she was spiritually, mentally, and emotionally. I could see bits and pieces of hurt escaping through her words and her tears. It was obvious to me her defense mechanisms were kicking in to protect her from feeling too beat-up and depressed. Listening to Julie tell her story, I was sure something was missing in her.

As Julie and I chatted, Jesus began speaking to me. It was through a simple nudge on my heartstrings, a hard-to-describe whisper in my spiritual gut. It wasn't a huge production; just a simple split-second thought that ran through my mind.

Bring peace to Julie's life; let her come live with you in Nashville.

When I felt those words in my heart, I figured it must have been a mistake. I assumed I must not have heard Jesus correctly. He couldn't have said that. Apparently, Jesus realized that I was struggling with doubt, because he repeated his words again:

Let Julie come live with you in Nashville.

How is that supposed to work, God?

You're going to sleep in the living room, and Julie is going to have your room. It won't be easy, but peace will come.

beatitude

I panicked a little: *Julie come live with me? What is God thinking?* The idea seemed preposterous to me. She's a girl. I'm a boy. *We're not married.* What would that look like? But I was almost positive I heard Jesus correctly. In the back of my mind, I was thinking about how I had always been told that Jesus frowned on guys and girls living together—you know—the whole "appearance" of evil. Too afraid that I might have heard Jesus wrong, I needed to test my hearing.

So, I decided I would try out Jesus's words on my mother. If my mom said no, I'd know that my fiancée would say no too. Oh yeah, I forgot to mention I was *engaged.* By then, I was pretty convinced Jesus was *out of his mind.*

That evening, after talking with Julie, I asked my mom about Jesus's crazy little idea. I expected her to think it was an absolutely ridiculous concept; how could she think otherwise? She was going to look at me and say, "*Matthew Turner,* you're out of your mind." So, while Mom was doing the dishes (she's a little easier to convince when she's doing something), I popped the question . . .

"*I think that's an awesome idea,*" my mother said.

I was shocked.

"Matthew, I think that might be the best thing for Julie! You definitely should!"

What?! I was floored that my mom, who was the stereotype of an overchurched, conservative woman—minus the tendency to be an ugly dresser—was actually receptive to Jesus's idea. In fact, my mom didn't just think the idea was good; she *loved* the idea.

"You and Julie have been friends for years; she's like your sister. It's a perfect plan, and I think it will really help her."

But Mom's acceptance of the idea only meant that I *had* to talk with Jessica (then my fiancée) about it, and I had no idea how she would respond. Later that night, over the phone (she lived in Wisconsin at the time), I posed the idea.

"Let me get this straight," said Jessica. "You want to let *Julie,* your best friend since you were three, sleep in your bedroom for three months? And you're going to sleep in the living room?"

"Umm, yeah," I said back to her. "I feel like Jesus wants me to do this. But I won't do it unless I have your support."

"So, while I'm living seven hundred miles away from you, you're going to have your friend, who is a girl, living with you?"

"Riiight."

"And you're sure this idea is from Jesus?"

"I believe it is, hon."

"Truthfully, I'm not too excited about it," she said. "But if you think it's what Jesus wants you to do, I'll support you through it. I might not always be happy about it, but I'll always support you, Matthew Paul Turner."

I knew with all my heart that Jessica meant that—*all of it.* Whenever she calls me by my full name she *really* means what she is saying. Not only did she believe in me, I was certain deep down inside her heart she hated the idea. But she was willing to give peace a chance.

So, one month later, Julie moved in. And I have to be honest; it wasn't always easy. In fact, at times, it was downright difficult—for her and for me. But the change in scenery and people and church life brought peace to Julie's life. Jesus simply asked me to be the conduit of peace for Julie. I don't say that proudly; I simply recognize the truth that I heard Jesus correctly that afternoon on the porch.

Sometimes, in order to live the way Jesus intends for me to live, I have to break a few rules. They're not always my rules. Sometimes they're the rules of a particular church. Sometimes they're the rules of friends or family. Sometimes they're simply rules that I have assumed to be true all of my life. But when I'm engaged in the journey, Jesus often surprises me by breaking a few rules.

When you're following after Jesus with abandon, you never know quite what you'll experience. Sometimes it will be a quiet, scenic ride. While other times it will reek of chaos and violence and intrigue. Making peace is certainly like that. In the movie *The Weather Man*, starring Nicholas Cage, Michael Caine plays the weatherman's father, and in a very interesting scene, he says, "Usually the right thing to do is always the hardest thing to do."

It more often than not seems that way for me. Jesus walks into my life and makes me do a lot of hard things, things I frankly don't understand some of the time. But I know for my friend Julie, that hard thing helped her find peace. And at the end of the day, helping somebody find a little peace brings you peace too. Sure, my simple actions are not ridding the world of war or famine or the other things in life I wish would go away. But when I'm helping someone experience the magical presence of Jesus through peace, I'm letting him work through me, and in the process I'm doing exactly what he intended for me to do. And perhaps, I'm giving someone else a chance to experience a little bit of the magic Jesus does in the lives of humans.

From time to time, I see my protesting friend online. She's still passionately rallying for peace every chance she gets. Despite not exactly understanding the method to her madness, I told her I was still very proud of her. I also admitted her love of peace had actually put me on my own journey toward trying to be more intentional with my peacemaking. But I told her I was doing it a little differently—the rally I got going on is not on the streets of Washington DC, instead it's going on inside my head and my heart.

peace

"I bet you I know who showed up at that peace rally," she wrote, trying to be smart.

"LOL," I wrote back. "Yeah, he showed up with a *big* sign that said, 'I am peace; I am peace. I am here to kill the beast.'"

"Ha-ha. Very funny! You shouldn't make fun."

"☺"

2

---

salt

Nobody likes having salt rubbed into their wounds,
even if it is the salt of the earth.

Rebecca West, English writer

Piece of Cake

My entire family was excited that my grandmother was preparing
one of her famous hot milk cakes for my seventh birthday party. I
loved my grandmother's hot milk cakes; she always smothered them
with homemade caramel frosting. On the afternoon of my birthday
party, she had worked the better part of an afternoon making my
cake. The finished product looked beautiful. As the family sang
"Happy Birthday" to me later that evening, my mother walked out
into the dining area with my candlelit birthday cake and placed
it right in front of me. My taste buds danced just thinking about
my grandmother's cake.

When they had finished singing, I held my breath long, made a silly wish I'm sure, and blew out the seven candles with all of my might. Everyone applauded. My mom pulled the candles out of the cake. She began to cut the cake into slices and put each slice on my special Flintstones happy birthday plates. My sister piled two scoops of vanilla ice cream next to the cake. And then she handed the plates out to the rest of the family.

For some reason, I remember my aunt Jean getting the first piece. She quickly and excitedly poked her fork into the cake and took a mouthful.

"*Oh, my word!*" exclaimed my aunt as if she had just tasted cow excrement. She shook her head in disgust as she spit out the cake into her napkin. "*Mother!* What did you do to this cake?"

My aunt Jean's boisterous tone alerted us all to stop what we were doing. Everyone in the room looked up. My mom stopped cutting slices of cake. My sister stopped serving the ice cream. I stared longingly at my cake and ice cream.

Perplexed by Aunt Jean's question, my grandmother took a small bite of her cake and instantly and quickly grabbed the closest napkin and spit it back out.

"Oh, Jean," said my grandmother, with frustration in her voice, "it tastes like I put salt in the batter instead of sugar. How on earth did I make that mistake? The sugar container looks nothing like the salt container. I *feel* horrible."

Large tears welled up in her eyes as the weight of throwing a kink into my large birthday gathering washed over her. My grandmother hated making mistakes like that; it reminded her that she was getting old and that her mind wasn't working like it used to.

I was only seven years old, but my mammom and I were close. I loved her dearly. I walked over and gave her a big hug.

"Can we still eat your cake, Mammom?" I whispered in her good ear.

"My goodness, no! Matthew, I am so sorry; too much salt makes something like a cake taste awful!"

Over the years, I have learned that salt is a very cumbersome ingredient. Too much salt ruins a lot more than just birthday parties.

Salt of the Earth

Jesus compares me, his follower, to salt. I think I like the concept of being compared to something as simple as salt. I like to use the words "I think" because I'm not too sure what I would have thought if he had compared me to oregano or paprika or some other kind of notable spice rack commodity. I'm sure I would have gotten used to the idea of being called the "paprika of the earth," but I'm not sure—mainly, because I'm not convinced paprika even has a purpose for being in my spice rack. Other than the fact that a little dash of it accents potato salad with a pretty red glow, what else is it good for?

But the fact I'm called to be like salt to the world is enthralling to me. Because unlike curry or oregano, salt isn't a flavor; it's a substance used to enhance flavor. (Duh, right?) In most cases, we don't put salt on something to make it taste different; we put salt on something in hopes it will help bring out the true flavor of whatever is being eaten.

Jesus has taught me he compares me to salt to give me an inkling of an idea of why I am here on earth. I'm not the flavor; I'm simply here to enhance the flavor. The "God-flavors," as Eugene Peterson so elegantly puts it, already exist here on earth; it's my job (and yours, too, if Jesus means something to you) as the "salt of the earth" to reveal his flavors, to bring them out, to enhance the Jesus-experience for others. In other words, we live to bring more notoriety to God's existence in our everyday circumstances.

What I most love about this truth is it means this: God is already here in the midst of whatever it is I will experience. I just need to help make him known. And when I make God known through seasoning the world around me with glimpses of his love and grace and mercy, I am doing exactly what I'm called to do.

Unfortunately, just like my grandmother's hot milk cake, I've learned too much salt overpowers all the other flavors. It takes over. Sometimes I have a tendency to bring my own version of Jesus into a situation, instead of recognizing he is already there. Consequently, instead of my actions enhancing Jesus, my words end up being too much, and it ends up making a potentially sweet piece of cake gross and bitter to the taste buds of others.

Sadly, too often I'm guilty of being a spiritual salt lick. On so many occasions, I have worn my faith so obtrusively that, when people see it, the idea of following Jesus is gross and unimaginable. The times I have ventured down this path, I have failed to enhance the God-flavors of this world. Instead, my "salt" overwhelms, and usually somebody is left with a very disgusting taste in their mouths. And high blood pressure ensues.

An Early Lesson in Being Salt

When I entered college in the fall of 1991, Jesus seemed to be more like a CEO to me than a father, friend, or Savior. My salvation then was systematic, built around an equation. I memorized a certain doctrine's vision statement; I followed its code of conduct and did my best to be a good employee of the Christian company of faith. My senior year in high school, I received "The Most Christ-Like Award." I guess you could say I was employee of the year; I even got a plaque with my name on it. I hung it up in my room, right next to "The Pastor's Award" I had received the year before.

Today, that kind of thinking seems so very distant to me. The last fifteen years have shown me very different pictures of Jesus than those I held on to as a young college student. But despite all of the time and life which separates who I am today from the naïve, young believer I once was, sometimes I still feel the heartbreak of what that kind of spiritual enterprise left behind. Mainly, I think about the people who I affected when I displayed to them my ugly, rigid version of Jesus. Sure, I was eventually able to break free of legalism, but when I think of the many disasters that I left in my path as I stood firmly and dependently on a skewed version of the truth, I can't help but ache for those I met along the way. (You'll read many stories in this book about that.) Over the years, I have often prayed for those poor individuals I tried to evangelize during that time.

While taking a business statistics class, I met Janet, who was a twenty-five-year-old nonpracticing Catholic, and Zachary, who was a twenty-year-old outspoken atheist. Before then, I had never met an atheist, and I had been taught all Catholics were going to hell. In my church, the word *Catholic* was derogatory. People would always frown or shake their head in utter sadness if an individual said they went to the Catholic church. When Janet informed me she was Catholic, my heart sank as my mind drew up images of her soul burning in hell. But those images paled in comparison to what I thought about Zachary after he told me he didn't believe there was a God at all. In my mind, I linked him with all of the other people who I believed were the great enemies of the Christian faith—Jezebel, the Philistines, JFK, and Hilary Clinton.

beatitude

The experience of community college overwhelmed me at first. Because I had lived most of my young life inside the bubble of church, Christian school, and a church-centered family, I had never gotten a chance to see what happened on the "other" side. But at community college, I quickly found out. My first day there, I left the school in tears. I was overwhelmed by talk of drunken parties, hearing the f-word *three* times, and the fact one of my professors was a "flaming liberal."

Although I had been spiritually programmed to respond to the "world's" challenges with scriptural answers, I felt rather unprepared and, quite frankly, out of my league. I had spent fifteen years studying under strict preaching. I was taught to be frank about my faith, intolerant of others' thoughts, and firm about holding true to my doctrinal belief system. My thoughts about Jesus and faith had never been challenged. So, when I was introduced to what I considered debauchery at Chesapeake College, I freaked.

"I'm *surrounded* by sinners," I told a friend of mine in utter desperation.

"Matthew, you will be surrounded by sinners for the rest of your life," he replied with pride. "Don't let them get the best of you. Just defend your faith. 'The Word of God is sharper than any two-edged sword.' Use it."

My friend's words impressed me. I had learned many times Christians were called to be the salt of the earth. My pastor had taught on that verse often. He said the Gospel message we're called to spread should burn the wounds of our enemies, and sometimes it would be bitter tasting to their lips. I went back to college believing that I needed to be prepared for any spiritual challenge that might come my way. And, over the next few weeks, I believed I had managed to prepare myself for "war." However, one conversation with Janet and Zachary proved otherwise.

"Why do you always have a Bible with you?" asked Janet one day after class.

"I like reading it between classes, so I keep it with me all of the time," I said—*frankly*. "We Christians believe the Bible is the Word of God, so it's important we know it."

Zachary laughed as he put his cigarette out on the cement steps where we were sitting. "It's just a bunch of stories, Matthew. Learn your history; there is absolutely no good evidence that supports God 'inspired' that book. And by the way, it's one of the most poorly written books in history. I think it's folklore."

My heart raced as Zachary's words rubbed up against my doctrinal vision statement. I had always heard about people like Zachary, ones who believed that the Bible was simply a book of fairy tales, but I had never heard anyone say it out loud.

"Well, that's *your* belief," I replied. "And it's not *poorly* written. *Again*, that's your belief. And you might want to be careful how quickly you belittle the Word of God."

"I'm not the only one who believes the Bible is a bunch of crap, Matthew," said Zachary, rolling his eyes and lighting up again. "In fact, some of the world's most intelligent people believe the Bible is nothing more than man's creation. I feel sorry for people like you—you're basing your entire life on stories that *never* happened."

The more he talked, the more his words made me sick to my stomach. It felt as though he had just poked me with a venomous needle, and the poison was working its way through the rest of my body.

"These are not just stories!" I said in a whispered holler. "This is *God's Word*, whether you believe it or not. And besides, nothing you say is going to change my mind."

Janet flicked her cigarette against the building as hard as she could.

"Oh, would both of you just shut up? I'm sick of hearing it." Janet had been uncomfortably listening to the discussion that *she* had started. "I wish to hell I had not brought it up. We can believe what we want to believe; that's what makes the world go around. Let's leave it at that."

Zachary stared at the ground and just let his cigarette burn slowly.

I looked at Janet, thinking to myself that her kind of thinking was going to get her a one-way ticket to destruction. *What do I do? Was I going to let God's Word get mocked by some well-read atheist punk and a Catholic?*

"I got one more thing to add," I said nervously, but loudly. I looked at them intently, like a judge looks at a man he's getting ready to sentence to life in prison. "I pity you both. What are you living for? All I see is two people who are simply living for themselves. You think you're smart, and you think you're cool, but when it comes to heaven or hell, all of that means absolutely nothing. Jesus said, 'I am the way, the truth, and the life.' *Period.* I believe if the two of you don't get saved and believe in Jesus, you'll live forever in—"

"OK, I've had enough!" said Janet, putting a book back into her book bag. "I've been hearing that same s—— from my old fart of a priest since I was six years old . . ."

I hardly heard what Janet was saying to me. I could feel my blood rushing away from my face as the feeling of embarrassment poured through every crevice of my body.

". . . I don't believe it. I think if you're a good person, you will get to heaven. And if I don't get to heaven, who cares? Hell is probably a whole lot more fun anyway."

Zachary looked at me and laughed. "You know what I believe, but thanks for the sermon."

They walked off together. As they made their way across the campus grounds, I watched them shake their heads and continue to laugh.

I was left there with one pounding thought burning inside: *My pastor was right, sometimes salt burns.*

I don't know where Janet and Zachary are now. I would love to be able to have the chance to apologize for making the "cake" too salty. But I can't—that was fourteen years ago.

You are the salt of the earth. But if the salt loses its saltiness, how can it be made salty again? It is no longer good for anything, except to be thrown out and trampled by men.

Matthew 5:13 NIV

A Silly Story about Stinking Up a Room

While sitting in my eighth-grade English class one afternoon, something smelled. It was a strong smell, and it seemed to be all around me. I tried to ignore it, but I couldn't. I kept getting not-so-subtle whiffs of it every few minutes. The awful smell was a mixture of scents—it seemed to be close to the smell of cooked sauerkraut that my mom would try and make me eat, but it was combined with the scent of an exotic type of cheese that I had only smelled and never tasted.

As I sat there trying my best to ignore it, I kept thinking to myself, *Where is this coming from?* As nonchalantly and as secretively as possible, I tried to smell all of the other kids who were around me to see if they were the culprits. But I was pretty sure it wasn't them. *Where is it coming from? Wow, this is horrible!* I tried as hard as I could to simply pay attention to my teacher's lesson, but it was difficult.

Toward the middle of my English teacher's lecture on the amazing prepositional phrase, he asked the class a question. Just as I was raising my hand to answer the question, I turned my head to the left to see if anyone else was raising their hands, and low and behold my nose caught the strongest whiff of that exotic cheese and sauerkraut aroma. *What the . . . ?!*

Before my teacher could call on me, I immediately put my hand down and began to smell *again* in that general direction. *Oh, my gosh, it's me who smells.* As I listened to someone else answer incorrectly the question that I knew, I sat at my desk and began to panic with questions: *I am the one who is stinking like my idea of the meal from "h" "e" double hockey sticks? It can't be. I'm probably the cleanest person here.*

The mere thought that this awful scent could be coming from my armpits was damaging my pride quickly. The scent that I had so affectionately labeled "the pollutant" was coming from *my* body. I could not believe my nose.

As my teacher continued talking about the powerful presence that a prepositional phrase brings to a sentence, I had a thousand thoughts racing through my mind: *Does anyone else smell me? Did I smell like this yesterday? Have people been talking about my stench behind my back? Why didn't my mother tell me my body would eventually do this? She usually tells me everything! How on earth am I going to make this go away?*

It was truly a horrible predicament to be in.

At the end of class, my teacher was handing back our graded spelling tests. All of us were huddled in a group waiting for him to call out our names so we could reach out our arms and take our tests. But I didn't want to lift up my arm. I felt unclean—like *leprosy* unclean. I was scared to death someone would notice that I stunk. But since I was much shorter than my teacher, I had no choice but to lift up my arm in the middle of that crowded group of beautiful smelling kids.

"Matthew T.," called my teacher.

I held my breath and reached up my arm and tried to grab that test as fast as I possibly could. And as soon as I could touch it, I thought for sure I was in the clear.

But I thought too soon.

"*Oh, my gosh!*" said Billie Joe, one of the girls in my school who thought she was supercool, and who, of course, always smelled quite nice. "Somebody has some *serious* B.O.!"

B.O.? What's B.O.? I felt relieved. I don't have B.O.; I just stink.

But my relief quickly passed when I saw that Billie Joe was holding her nose with two fingers and crinkling her nose. And, of course, like most eighth-grade girls, she didn't just make her comment and then stop talking. She continued to talk—*loudly.*

"*Who stinks?*" she asked again. "*Somebody* needs to buy some deodorant. *Mr. Waters, tell whoever stinks to buy some deodorant. Oh, it's just awful!*"

I didn't know what to do. Does she know it's me? It was all happening so fast that I could barely tell. Had she been looking for an opportunity like this to tell me that I stink? I began to panic—more! Come on, Mr. Waters; just dismiss the class!

The longer I stood there, the more paranoid I became that Billie Joe knew it was me. She had to. I was standing right next to her. I had pretty much just placed my unhairy, unguarded armpit in her pretty, made-up face when she screamed the comment to the entire room. But suddenly a genius idea came to me. I decided that I would make a comment about the stinky person too.

I mean, if the person joins in with the teasing, everyone's going to assume that it's *not* him. *Right?* So, that's what I did. I blurted out a comment.

"Billie Joe, you're right! Somebody *does* stink in here," I said, as convincingly as I could.

Boy, did that statement turn my "perfectly doable Tom Cruise" kind of problem into an "oh, my gosh, what the crap am I going to do Robert Downey Jr." kind of problem. I should have kept my mouth closed. Because still to this day, I can hear her toxic words ringing in my ear.

"It's *you, Matthew Turner!*" she screamed, again at the top of her lungs, pointing right at me. *"You're* the one who *stinks! You need to buy some deodorant."*

And then she sang, "You need to buy some deodorant," five times over.

Instantly, I felt two inches tall. My eighth-grade face turned a thousand shades of white. I just stared at her in terror. I instantly began praying that Jesus would do all kinds of bad things to her.

But I said nothing. I had already said enough. So, I just stood there trying desperately to hold back the tears that were beginning to form in the corners of my eyes. And then, while the others in the classroom laughed hysterically at my misfortune and Billie Joe reveled in her newly appointed spotlight, I grabbed my test and walked out of the room.

It's hard when suddenly, for the first time, your nose is open to your own stench. It's embarrassing. You think to yourself, *Is that really me? Am I really the one who's smelling up this room? Have people smelled my scent before? Will I ever live down this moment when my armpits were the center of everyone's attention? When I walk in this room tomorrow smelling like a GQ ad, will anyone even notice that I made a change? Will I get a second chance? Will people ever want to smell me again?*

On that day, as I rode the bus home from school, the questions consumed me.

Sometimes I ask the same kinds of questions about the times I have over-"salted" my words and actions with evangelical hype. Will those people trust me again? Will they be willing to listen to my *new* stories, the ones that don't have to be overloaded with jargon or a mean-spirited tone or Jesus one-liners? Will people ever want to *smell* me again?

It wasn't until several years after meeting Zachary and Janet at my community college that I actually began to smell the stench of my words and tone in that conversation. The aroma hit me out of nowhere. Just like realizing my armpits stunk in eighth grade, I recognized the stink of my bad attempts at being "salt." I hear the memory of smell is long. My college acquaintances, Janet and Zachary, never came back for another whiff. On second thought, neither did Billie Joe.

I'm not sure what it is about following Jesus that has made me act so weird and awkward and sometimes downright stupid. Is it because at times I *think* I know it all? Is it an inner need to make people understand me? But I'm not alone. Most of the weirdest things I have encountered in my life have "Christian" written on them. As with my case as a college student, the stench of Christians is revealed more through evangelism than anything else. I smell it often, the scent of misplaced words and poor, unexcusable timing. When mixed with uninterested patrons, it becomes an especially nasty odor.

I was recently on a public bus in Denver. I was there on business, but one afternoon I managed to get away and see the downtown sights. While riding public transportation, I witnessed two local Colorado women stumble into a conversation with a thirty-something businessman who was in Denver on business from Atlanta. The conversation began as most conversations do—a friendly hello, a common interest in the weather, and a mutual love for something—this time it was for the city of Atlanta.

As I watched this conversation begin from the seat across the aisle, I couldn't help but eavesdrop. It's always fascinating for me to watch other people interact. Even before I knew where this conversation was heading, the fact that this clean-cut looking man with a flair for dressing was engaging in a conversation with two local women looking as if they were on their way downtown for a few beers was, to say the least, a writer's dream come true.

After the "new friends" ended their chitchat, I noticed the man was pulling something out of his pocket. At the time, I wasn't sure what it was, but it was, to him, something important. Then, a couple of minutes later, the man cleared his throat and spoke. His tone was nervous, as if he was unprepared for what he was about to say. And quite honestly, his nervousness didn't seem to fit him.

"So, can I ask you ladies a question? Are you two Christian women?" he asked. "I don't mean to be so forward, but . . ."

Wow. That was a gutsy question, indeed. And to me, it was quite unnecessary. I mean, from my vantage point, these two women had every stereotypical quality of lesbians. And they didn't seem like Jesus-loving lesbians. Their short spiked hair was about as close to mullets as you can get and still be considered somewhat cool anywhere outside of West Virginia. Their clothes were masculine looking—baggy jean shorts and simple T-shirts. And one was still wearing her "Vote for Howard Dean" T-shirt despite the fact that W had won nine months prior. Sure, they maybe weren't gay, but at that point, I would have bet a pretty good amount of money on the fact that the two women were *together*.

"No, we're not Christians," laughed the woman wearing the Howard Dean T-shirt. She then looked at her friend and smiled. "We don't like religion too much."

Without skipping a beat, the businessman continued talking.

"Well, ladies, I know we don't have a lot of time, but I firmly believe I would be doing you a disservice if I didn't share with you my heart for Jesus," said the Christian man. "You see, I believe the Bible teaches that we are all sinners—"

"Sir," interrupted the woman who was *not* wearing the Howard Dean T-shirt, "we're really not interested in hearing this. We're not trying to be rude, but I think we'll both be OK without hearing your Jesus story."

The Christian man never blinked an eye. He looked down at the piece of paper that he had pulled out of his coat pocket and looked to be scanning it quickly. He then spoke again.

"Well, if you would be so kind as to just give me one more moment of your time, I would love to simply tell you why I believe in Jesus. You see, he is one day going to judge us all, ladies. And I don't believe it's going to be too long before it happens. It says in Romans 3 . . ."

I sat there worried for this man's life as he simply ignored these two women's request. They fidgeted. They stopped looking in his direction. They rolled their eyes toward me. They gave every indication they wanted to be off the bus as quickly as possible. But he kept right on talking. And his knowledge of Scripture was impressive. He could seemingly quote many Bible verses about our need for God's salvation.

"Sir," said the Howard Dean lover, "if you don't stop talking to us, we're going to move away from you. Can you please stop?"

"Yes, ma'am," said the businessman. "But let me give you this pamphlet on how you can learn more about being a Christian just in case you're interested. My phone number is at the bottom, and if you need . . ."

Just as he was handing them the Jesus information he had pulled out of his pocket, the bus driver called the women's stop. I wasn't sure if it was *their* stop or if it was simply the *next* stop. They took the piece of paper and walked off the bus. One of them was laughing hysterically; the other was shaking her head in disgust. I watched them as they walked down the street. Miss "Howard Dean" took the Jesus information and tore it in two and threw it in a garbage can. Luckily, I don't believe the business-man saw that.

At the next stop, the businessman got off the bus. As he passed close by me, he handed me one of his pamphlets and said, "Glory to God. He's good, ain't he?"

Another person on the bus looked at me and called him a "nutcase."

He is a nutcase, I thought. But I felt guilty for thinking that.

When I experience events like this one, I want to run up to the would-be recipients and say to them not *all* people who pursue lov-ing Jesus are like this. I want to tell them we think people like Pat Robertson and the folks on TBN are sometimes a little weird too. I would want them to know we, too, see how God gets thrown into the cultural agenda—by politicians, preachers, and the like—to seemingly be used to promote an agenda or manipulate people.

But most of the time, almost every time, I remain silent, para-lyzed by fear.

Walking with Jesus has taught me I don't need to make those

opinions known unless I'm talking to a very close friend. I believe if I were to blurt those thoughts out to just anybody, it would be just as stench-stricken as obnoxious evangelism. I believe it would be hypocritical and conceited. I believe Jesus, in his power, takes care of situations where Christians add too much salt.

He's certainly had to take care of many situations where I have made him look foolish and ugly. Salt sometimes does that, you know?

Salt against the Tongue

I wish you could know Brian Bowdren. I met him in 1997.

The man I speak about might be one of the most intriguing people I've had the pleasure of knowing. When I met him, he was forty-three and seemed almost perfect to me. Something about Brian made everyone who met him want to, and perhaps feel like they needed to, emulate his actions.

He had an addictive nature that people found attractive.

Brian had an amazing job, one which took him all over the United States and other parts of the world. His trips would often put him in front of high-profile people of influence, power, and wealth. Brian was talented and creative; his love of playing bass guitars led him to open a music shop in his quaint hometown on the Eastern Shore of Maryland, where he handcrafted bass guitars and sold them on eBay. Brian was in shape; he had a daily workout routine that kept his muscular body somewhere between 4 and 5 percent body fat. He was the kind of guy who made you kind of sick to your stomach.

Whenever I heard his wife, Cindy, talk about him, I had to stop and listen. Her love, respect, and adoration for her husband was something out of legend. She hated to be away from him. In fact, when our church would have weekend women's retreats,

Cindy would go to the program during the day but never stay overnight. On one such occasion, I asked her why. Her reply made me smile. "Because I get to sleep next to Brian Bowdren; why would I ever want to miss a chance to do that?" she said with a coy grin.

Brian was an elder at his church. He was on the boards of several ministries. He was well-read. He played bass guitar in his church's praise and worship band. Most Christians who met him were surprised to learn Brian had only come to know Jesus when he was in his midthirties. To many, that just didn't seem possible.

I got to know Brian when he was one of my bosses at Jammin' Java. When we first met him, I wanted to have a job like Brian's. I wanted to be talented like Brian. I wanted a marriage like Brian's. But after spending three years watching this man's interaction with people, I wanted to bring out the God-flavors of the earth like Brian.

Brian worked out his salvation by relating to people. I never once witnessed a person he couldn't relate to. When he would sit in board meetings with the elite of society, he was eloquent and masterful. Despite not being considerably *moved* or *impassioned* by his nine-to-five, that did not stop him from investing his complete self into his work and the relationships he created. He understood his job was a part of the platform where Jesus wanted him to live out his faith. On a couple of occasions, I watched as some of the smartest and richest men and women of this world responded to Brian's good nature, love of life, and faith in someone much bigger than himself.

But Brian was far from one-dimensional. At the guitar shop/Christian coffeehouse where we worked side by side, I witnessed Brian also relating to people who were much different than him—the poor, the unintelligent, the exotic, the liberal, and the outcasts.

It didn't matter if he was talking to an atheist, a gothic-prone kid, or a dumb jock; Brian was always the same. He never once tried to talk over them or belittle them with his intelligence, even though I couldn't help but laugh when I witnessed certain conversations where his brain was struggling to dumb down large concepts into digestible language. His willingness to invest in people was uncanny to me. It was unrehearsed and never seemed forced. It was simply a part of who he was as a person, a person who was trying desperately to love Jesus. And he did that by loving people.

However, I believe it was in the relationships of those Brian loved the most that I realized what Jesus meant when he said, "You are the salt of the earth." I witnessed him shopping for dresses for his wife when there wasn't any holiday or anniversary to celebrate. On many occasions, Cindy would walk into church looking stunning. I'd tell her how pretty she looked that morning, and almost every time she would say, "Oh, I can't take any credit for this; Brian bought this for me."

"Was it for your birthday?" I'd ask.

"No, just because he loves me."

That was Brian.

I heard secondhand about how his words and wisdom helped our pastor during a difficult time.

I watched him encourage his Sunday school class to dive deeper in their faith.

A friend of mine said that he wouldn't be playing drums if it weren't for Brian.

Another told me that he wouldn't have a relationship with Jesus if it weren't for Brian.

I'm actually pretty darn sure I wouldn't be writing this book if it weren't for Brian's investment in me.

beatitude

The manner in which Brian lived his life had a way of bringing out the best in people.

It saddens me that I have to write about Brian's life in the past tense. In December 2004, Brian died suddenly of unexplained causes. While working on a brand-new bass guitar that he had designed and created by hand, he collapsed. His wife discovered his body an hour or so later. An autopsy was performed, but it never explained the whys behind his early death. He was fifty.

Despite his passing, I still taste the God-flavors Brian seasoned with his life on earth. Many do. But Brian wasn't perfect. He fought the same battles all of us do when we grapple with the idea of Jesus calling us salt. Staying out of God's way and allowing the mysteries of Jesus to shine through his life did not come naturally. Humility wasn't natural for him. Talking to the uneducated wasn't always simple for him. He wasn't *always* happy, and he didn't always have the perfect Jesus-answer to offer people. Often surprising to me, he was overtly honest about not fully understanding everything about Jesus. Brian didn't believe he had to. To him, that was what faith was all about—believing in something he couldn't see. It only seemed logical to him that he would not be able to fully understand what he could not see with his eyes. To Brian, following Jesus wasn't about having all the answers; it was about simple obedience in the everyday.

Brian felt the call to be salt in the world. One day, while drinking coffee and eating scones together, he looked at me with his humble eyes, and with his raspy voice he said, "Find the thread of Jesus in every story you live, Matthew . . . we're not here to master this life; *we can't* master this life. We're here to use our own stories and journeys and struggles and joys to make those watching us see a glimpse of Jesus's story for their lives. I just try to live my life to the fullest," Brian said, seeming somewhat careful with his words. "And then I pray that God will use me in the story."

Brian laughed quietly, and then added, "I know he doesn't need me, but it's always good fun to be a part of what God is doing in the lives of other people."

To those of us who still benefit from Mr. Brian's God-story, the God-filled taste on our tongue is nothing less than magical.

3

heart

*Great beauty, great strength, and great riches are really
and truly of no great use; a right heart exceeds all.*

Benjamin Franklin

No, Maybe, Sure

When I was a kid, my youth pastor made pursuing a pure heart
sound pretty simple. "Deny the flesh," he'd tell us nearly every
Sunday morning. "Be careful what your eyes see. Be careful what
your ears hear." At thirteen, I believed my youth pastor was cor-
rect; staying pure *was* easy, especially when most of your world
still revolved around getting to the next level of a Super Mario
Brothers video game. But for some reason, getting older seemed
to complicate all of that. It complicated that a lot, really.

Just before my sixteenth birthday, I was introduced to a whole
new world of possibilities. On April 25, 1989, I got into the back-

seat of a blue beat-up driver's ed car. A friend of mine and I were taking the driving class together. While I was waiting for my turn to practice driving on the highway, my friend took his turn behind the wheel. Our instructor, a Hispanic guy named Maurice, worked for his father who owned and ran the driving school.

When we were finally safely driving on the highway, Maurice began looking through his tape collection for music to play. This excited me. It wasn't too often that I was able to listen to real music, especially the kind with guitar solos and drums. My church said guitar solos made Satan dance.

"How do you guys like your music?" asked Maurice with a wink.

"Um, I really don't know that much rock music," I replied. "So, you should just play whatever you want to play."

"Oh, whatever," said Maurice, pulling out one of his two hundred cassettes that were organized by release date in a huge carrying case. "You'll *definitely* know this song."

Maurice didn't get it. My friend and I were fundamentalist Baptists. We had been taught since we were five that his kind of music delivered us right into the hands of evil. We were supposed to run as fast as we could from such evil. But at the time, I chose to stay in the backseat.

"See if you guys know this song," said Maurice, shoving the tape into the player. He then turned his head toward me and gave me his best this-is-going-to-so-rock scrunched-up face. I remember thinking that *he* kind of looked like Satan.

"I don't know this song," I said as soon as I heard the first drumbeat.

"Give it a second to play, man," Maurice said. "You got to know this song! It's *everywhere*. B-104 plays it all the time."

"I don't *listen* to rock and roll!" I countered. "I'm not allowed to. I've never listened to B-104."

This was quite true; I was only allowed to listen to Christian music, and only if it didn't have drums. My church said that drums harnessed evil spirits.

"You guys have never heard this song? *Are you kidding?*" asked Maurice, acting as if the two of us Christian school kids were a freak show. "This is 'Pour Some Sugar on Me' by Def Leppard. This song rocks my socks off," said Maurice. "It's such a *nasty* little song."

Maurice sang the lyrics and shook his head to the beat every time the chorus came on.

"I cannot believe you have never heard this song," he continued. "Do you ever get to listen to any good music?"

That's when I asked him if he had ever heard of Amy Grant. He hadn't. I pretended like I was a big fan of hers. Of course, at the time, I was only allowed to listen to her slow stuff.

Determined, Maurice went through about ten tapes trying to find one song that he thought we might have heard. But he couldn't find one. I did tell him that I heard Michael Jackson's "Bad" on the Pepsi commercial once. He rolled his eyes.

"Wow. So you guys are pretty sheltered, huh?" he asked.

"I guess so, but we don't look at it like that. It's just who we are. We follow Jesus, and so, that means we stay away from rock music."

"Are you Amish?" he asked. "Cuz I have a friend who used to be Amish. But I guess he converted to 'heathen' when he was sixteen."

"No, we're not Amish," I replied. I was becoming less and less impressed with Maurice. But he kept asking my friend and me questions. Eventually, he began asking us about girls.

"You guys must not get much action with the ladies, huh?"

"I've held hands with a girl," said my friend.

"*What?!* That's all you've done? That's stinkin' hilarious, man.

Gosh, you don't know what you're missing. By the time I was sixteen, I had seen it all."

As I listened to Maurice ask my friend a hundred questions about his experiences, I was praying he wouldn't turn and do the same to me. The questions were personal and used words that I was allowed to use only in bathrooms and hospitals.

"So you two have never seen breasts," said Maurice with a laugh, like he already knew the answer to his question. He looked at me.

I quickly shook my head no.

Maurice laughed a big hearty laugh and then asked, "Do you want to?"

As soon as I had heard those words, my heart felt like it stopped beating in my chest.

Of course, my great influence of a friend quickly said, "Sure, I'll look at them!"

"How about you, Mr. Matt? You want to see 'em?" asked Maurice again, rather forcefully.

"That's OK; I don't think I want to see the pictures," I said with all the conviction I could muster up. But really, I was curious. Inside my naïve mind a vicious game of tug-of-war began between my desire to see a woman without clothes and the preaching that I had heard since I was five. *Keep your heart pure* kept running over and over in my head. *Run as fast as you can away from temptation.* I could feel the war happening within my spirit. *Satan's like a lion, and he wants to eat you alive.* But the curiosity of seeing those pictures was killing me. *I wonder what Joseph would do; he would drop everything and run.* A nervous excitement had worked its way through my bones. My young teenage senses were on overdrive. Sure I was saying no out loud, but inside, I was curious—*really* curious.

"Come on," said Maurice. "You know you want to see the pictures. God ain't gonna send you to hell for one little peek at some of the most beautiful breasts you will ever see."

"Matthew, it's no big deal," said my friend. "It's only some pictures."

"Yeah, man; I got them right here," said Maurice, opening his glove compartment. "Two magazines full of some very beautiful pictures of naked women doing some unbelievable things."

When I walked into school the next day, I realized that I had become quite unpopular overnight—because I had refused to look at the pictures. My friend, on the other hand, had become a star—Mr. Popularity in fact.

While I had driven the car that day, he had sat in the backseat and thumbed through those magazines. He had stories to tell. He had pictures to describe. He had gotten an inside look at what the world looked like on the other side. By the way most of the guys treated him, you would have thought he had just matured three years in twelve hours. Honestly, a part of me kind of envied him.

Many times over the next few months I wished I *had* looked at the pictures. My friend and his buddies had inside jokes about him seeing the pictures. I wasn't privy to the inside jokes. In fact, they purposefully left me out of them. And when you're in the tenth grade, is there anything more humiliating than being left out of an inside joke? At that time, I didn't think so.

My only solace from the entire situation was my heart had been left pure. I had stayed perfect. Because I had run from temptation, I thought I had kept my heart from being contaminated. But that changed.

Somehow, one of my teachers caught wind of the story and decided to talk with me after class one afternoon.

"I heard what happened a few weeks ago," he said, looking at me firmly.

"You did?" I asked, somewhat embarrassed a teacher had found out about me hearing rock music and almost looking at pictures of naked women. "Yeah, well," I said, "the last few weeks have been some of the worst of my life."

"I can imagine," said my teacher.

I listened to him intently despite the fact his bald head was reflecting a lot of light and making it hard to concentrate.

"Life is never simple when you make a decent choice, Matthew. Good choices often complicate things. People make fun. You're tempted to feel proud of yourself for making a good decision. It can be pretty rough."

"You don't think I should be proud of myself?" I asked.

"Nah, I don't think so," he said in a very pleasant voice. "In reality, you're really no better than the 'other guy.'"

"What? But I didn't look. *He looked!*"

"Yeah, I know you didn't look. But that's not what makes a heart pure. You wanted to, right?"

"Well, sure; I guess." I stopped talking for a second, and then I grinned. "Yes, I wanted to look. What guy wouldn't want to?"

"I figured," he said, obviously trying not to smile. "Matthew, always remember this."

My teacher looked at me like he was staring at a younger version of himself.

"You made a great choice a few weeks ago, but the opportunity for you to have made the bad choice still existed in your heart, buddy. And the fact you've walked around here for the last month or so like you're a little better than everyone else is just as sinful as looking at those pictures. Our hearts are naturally evil. Don't think for a second you are above that. I've made that mistake before."

My teacher's words hit me hard. They surprised my fifteen-year-old mind. When he stopped me after class and told me he knew the story,

I expected him to congratulate me, pat me on the back, and say, "Well done, you good and faithful servant." Instead, he put me on the same level as my friend. I know now my teacher could have gotten into a lot of trouble for having that conversation. He knew the story, yet he didn't report it. He talked to my friend, but he didn't punish him.

On that particular day, when my teacher spoke to me, I didn't get what he was trying to say. In fact, I didn't fully understand the wisdom he was communicating about the capability of my heart until I began truly traveling with Jesus many years later.

Today, every time I get a clear picture of what my heart is capable of, I think of what my teacher shared with me many years ago. Sure, when I make a good decision my heart escapes being filled with more junk. But the action in and of itself does not make my heart pure. Relearning Jesus has taught me my heart is capable of a lot; it's in my brokenness and humility that I see just how much. I didn't know that when I was fifteen. I think most fifteen-year-olds don't know this.

Two and a half years went by before I had *another* chance to see pictures of naked women. And that time, I looked. I pretty much jumped out of my skin for the chance to see something so beautiful and decadent. But unlike my friend's experience from a couple of years before, when I looked at pornography for the first time, my life didn't go from mediocre to fame and popularity overnight. When I experienced porn for the first time, I just felt a whole bunch of guilt. Guilt chased me like a lion chases a gazelle. And for much of my young adult life, I was eaten alive.

Only recently have I fully begun to understand the weight of that first encounter with pornography. Sure, when I looked at the women in those pictures that day, it sent my curiosity through the roof and gave my mind enough visual stimulant to rule my imagination for many months. But that's not all that happened.

That first encounter also created in me a false sense of security. It was a security that said to me, "If I stay away from pornography, my heart will be made good in the eyes of Jesus." So, that's what I did; well, that's what I tried to do. I poured every bit of spiritual and emotional energy into staying away from pornography.

The more I pursued trying to *feel* pure, the more I failed. And every time I failed, like clockwork, I would venture through the motions of trying to *make* Jesus deem me good again. I did that over and over and over again. Years went by (ten to be exact) before I realized my thinking was spiritually destructive. Eventually, I learned nothing I could do would make Jesus deem me good. Only he could make my heart good, and that was not something that would happen instantly.

Sure, I can create spiritual habits that will clean up my heart or keep it from getting mucked up by sin, but I can do nothing to make God deem it good. *That's* what my teacher was trying to tell me that day—if I depend on my own actions to make me pure, I would never see God.

I had read many times before that Jesus said a person with a pure heart sees God. Because I want to see God, probably more than any other spiritual thing, I have worked the hardest at trying to make my heart pure. I want to make it pure enough to see God. And not surprisingly, that battle has probably been the most complicated part of my Christian life. But because of my desire to see God, I keep walking with Jesus on the journey. And once in a while I do get a glimpse.

The Art of Seeing God

Some people who see God frighten me a little. I don't mean this in a mean-spirited way. It's just that I was raised in a church that believed Satan was behind every corner ready to pounce on me. And I tend to think that's a bit weird sometimes. But, as I've experienced Jesus, I have also met many Christians who think they can see God in absolutely everything. I wanted to believe it, but frankly, it was difficult. When one guy confessed to me that he believed he could see the face of God etched in his hardwood floor, I became a little skeptical. But one person I met took seeing God to a whole new level.

"I swear I can see him," said Angela to the new guy at work. Angela was a co-worker of mine at a company I worked for many years ago.

"I will tell you the story," she exclaimed quite excitedly.

"Angela, why don't you wait a few days or maybe even weeks before you tell that story?" I pleaded. "Give Dave a chance to get to know you first." Angela just glared at me from across the lunch table.

"Oh, don't stop her," said Dave, who had started working for the company only a few days before. "Who do you see, Angela?"

"Dave, I see Jesus in the *fluffy* white clouds," Angela said with delight. "When the sky is nothing but blue, with white clouds, I often take pictures, and when I get the pictures back, there's always one that overwhelms me with the face of Jesus."

I had only known Angela for a few months, but she frustrated me. She had a habit of always bringing up her God-sightings around the new people at work. She had more God-sightings than any person I had ever met in my life. She usually saw him in the clouds, but once in a while she would come in with pictures of trees, fields, and the occasional sunset and claim to see the divine. Whenever a new sighting occurred, she'd bring in her picture and then tell more than a few people in the office where she saw God or Jesus, and once in a while, even Mary. But as far as I could tell, nothing was ever in the picture which remotely resembled Jesus or anyone else holy for that matter.

Other than that little quirk, Angela was a *really* nice person. But she never gave anyone a chance to get to know her. It was almost as if she went out of her way to make people think she was a little bit strange. And honestly, she *was* a little strange. But for some reason, I found her to be a very innocent and pure soul. I guess most didn't take the time to see her in that light.

"Angela, come on now," said Shandi, who had been with the company for twelve years. "You know you don't see Jesus in the clouds."

"I do too," Angela insisted. "I think it's a gift. Look it up on the Internet. People have a gift for seeing God in things."

"You got about as much of a gift for seeing Jesus in the clouds as my fat a—— has of doing ten backflips down that hallway out there. And you know how likely that is."

Shandi's comment made everyone in the lunchroom laugh. I tried not to. But no such luck. Imagining Shandi's three-hundred-pound body doing backflips down the hallway *was* humorous.

"Go ahead and laugh," said Angela to everyone, but then she focused her attention on me. "Matthew, I am surprised at you joining in like that. You're the only other Christian in this room. You should be supporting me."

Every time Angela would get herself backed up in a corner, she would always use the Christian-sister excuse to try and guilt me into defending her. It worked almost every time.

"I'm not laughing at you, Angela," I said, trying to smooth things over a bit. "I'm laughing *with* Shandi. You have to admit, what she said was kind of funny."

"I want to see one of the pictures," said Dave.

"You do?" said Angela like a hyper seven-year-old kid.

By the time Dave had said the word "picture," she was already running toward the door.

"Oh, lord," said Shandi. "Now, you've done it, Dave. You'll never get her to shut up about Jesus now."

Angela returned a minute later with her picture in hand and flashed it for everyone to see.

"Oh! I like this one!" said Shandi sarcastically. "This is the one where I'm pretty sure I can see a big ole replica of my big butt in the clouds."

Shandi grabbed the picture from Angela's fingers and held it in front of Dave's face.

"Look here, Dave," yelled Shandi, pointing to a specific spot on the picture. "Can you see my butt right there between the cloud that looks like Tina Turner and the one that's kind of shaped like Felix the Cat?"

Shandi laughed obnoxiously.

"Give me my picture!" snapped Angela. "Dave, Jesus is right here."

Angela pointed to the spot on the picture where she truly believed she saw the face of Jesus. Although Dave couldn't see any deity in the picture, he never belittled her. He simply smiled.

Honestly, I had looked at the picture twenty times and prayed I would see Jesus, but I never did. I guess Angela had a purity of heart I didn't understand. Either that, or she was just insane.

Confession Is Good for the Eyes

Angela believed with all of her heart she saw Jesus in certain clouds. As stupid and unbelievable as that sounded to me, it was always hard to argue with Angela. Those sightings were such an avid part of her personality; she believed it with all of her heart. I could tell that she believed in her pictures of God almost as confidently as I believed Jesus to be my Savior. No amount of teasing, ridicule, or advice from me ever shut Angela up. No matter who it was, nearly everybody in the office had heard Angela's story once.

The sappy part of me wishes I could see Jesus in this life as easily as Angela did in the clouds.

People who see God—*really* see God—on a regular basis are sometimes intimidating to me. Their lifestyles and words rub up against mine. I don't feel judgment or guilt necessarily. At least, I don't feel that from them. It's my experience a pure heart doesn't reflect such things as judgment or impatience.

But sometimes I do have this sense of conviction and spiritual craving when I meet such a person (like my meeting with Henry Blackaby).

I believe a pure heart is one of the most beautiful and attractive qualities I have ever witnessed in a human being. It doesn't mean a person is perfect; it simply means they're willing to stay on the journey with Jesus for the long haul. They don't stop and make faith a destination. They know the path to a pure heart. They put what they know into practice.

My grandmother always taught me a pure heart happens when a person confesses often. For ten years I watched my grandmother pray. When she turned eighty-one, she moved in with my family. She shared a bedroom with my little sister. Some of the most profound lessons about Jesus I learned from watching her. (I explain her impact in my life further in the chapter on truth.) When Mammom prayed, she did it the old-fashioned way—kneeled beside her bed, hands in folded position resting on the bedspread, and her eyes were always closed. She told me once when she prayed at night, she'd always first ask Jesus to forgive her for all the sin she had committed that day. When we were kids, my sister and I always found this a little humorous.

"Mammom, what sins do you confess?" I asked her one time. "You seem perfect to me."

"Oh, you'd be surprised," she said in the most innocent of tones. "Sometimes when you see me smiling and having a good attitude, I'm only doing that on the outside to make people think I'm happy. But on the inside, I'm thinking all kinds of bad things."

"Really?" My fourteen-year-old head didn't buy it.

"Just last week, Jean told me something in confidence, and the very next day, I was on the phone with Regina telling her all about it," said my grandmother with a grin. Jean and Regina were Mammom's best friends.

My grandmother never wanted to miss a chance to see Jesus throughout her day.

"I know I forget some things," she'd say. "So, I always ask the Holy Spirit to come and help me remember. I haven't got the greatest memory you know."

My grandmother told me several times that when her heart was clean—not necessarily empty, not perfect—only then could she see God. And she did see him too. She didn't see his face in pictures like my co-worker Angela did; Mammom saw his presence in the circumstances of her life. And her life had sometimes been quite hard. She suffered a miscarriage early in her marriage. She lost Jack, her eleven-year-old son, to a ruptured appendix. She held her family together when my grandfather went through many years of depression and grief over Jack's death. She overcame a heart attack in her seventies. But when grace compelled her to confess daily, she was certain Jesus made her heart pure.

"Confession is the most beautiful of places that God can see our hearts," she said to me once, although I am most certain she stole that from one of the many radio preachers she would listen to in the mornings. Either way, something was always very clean and good and pure about my Mammom.

I'm Staring at a Pure Face Afraid to Ask a Question

One of my responsibilities as editor of *CCM* was to occasionally meet with new bands and hear their stories about why they chose to go into music. The experience was always a little formulaic and weird for me. I knew that their record label had set up the meeting hoping I would choose them for coverage in the magazine. The bands and artists would often feel pressure to put on their best "face" and to present their best stories for me to hear. It was no doubt as uncomfortable for them as it was for me at times.

One time I had lunch with a hard-core band. I was less than excited about this lunch—mainly because I was not a huge fan of hard-core music, but also because the magazine was on a deadline. And I needed to be working back at my office. When I arrived, I joined five guys who seemed to be trying desperately to look like hard rockers. I can't help but think that trying to look like Green Day is hard and awkward when you're Christian. Well, maybe it was just hard for me to witness a band trying too hard to play that part. It always seemed fake and rehearsed. When I sat down at the table, I tried desperately not to talk too much.

So, I just listened to their stories.

The two men who spoke the most were both thirty-year-olds; one was the lead singer. Their stories included drugs, sex, alcohol, an attempted suicide, and time in jail. They talked about God coming into their lives a few years back and his presence saving them and their families out of hopelessness. Their stories were dramatic and impressive from an evangelical standpoint. You could tell they had shared their stories often. They were perfectly told—almost like they were reading from a teleprompter.

But despite their stories having lots of drama, they were stories I had heard a hundred times before. I could certainly appreciate the extraordinary nature of what had occurred, but I wasn't *really* moved

heart

enough by their stories to consider them for a feature in the magazine. Two of the other band members shared short stories about being raised in Christian homes, making a few mistakes, and now being completely on fire for Jesus. Again, their stories were good, but they didn't spark a lot of interest from an editorial standpoint, either.

However, the entire time I was listening to the stories of those four men, something about the guy down at the far end of the table intrigued me. He had dark Mongolian skin. His hair was jet black and he wore it in dreads. His look was normal for a Christian rock band. I hadn't heard his story. In fact, only a few times during the conversation had he even spoken up. When he did, an unfettered innocence flowed from him. It wasn't in his words. We had *all* been sitting there chatting about the goodness of Jesus in our stories. But something about this guy was pure. He simply reeked of Jesus. My spiritual gut kept saying to me, *Let him tell you his story.*

But honestly, I fought it a little bit. I wasn't sure I wanted to hear what Jesus was doing in his life. I was afraid that this young man's *pure* story would somehow interfere and make my own seem worthless. I was afraid his innocence would make my story feel ugly, perverted, and trite. Being near him made me feel convicted; hearing his life story might make it worse. But Jesus wouldn't let me walk away without hearing him out.

We were getting close to the end of our time together and the young man still hadn't said much yet. So, I directed the conversation toward him.

"Dude," I said, looking at him, "are you *perfect*? There's just something about you I can't figure out."

The guys in the band started laughing hysterically.

"No, I'm being serious," I said, trying to get the others to be quiet. "There is just something very 'Christ-like,' for lack of a better term, about you. It's a spirit or something. I can't really explain . . ."

beatitude

"Matthew," said one of the other guys in the band, still laughing, "we're laughing because he gets that everywhere we go. People *always* identify Jesus in his life."

"Well, I can see why," I said, smiling, stumbling over my words a bit. "I'm sitting here feeling convicted by you. And *you* have hardly said anything."

"Tell him your story, man," coaxed the lead singer.

The young man spoke up. It wasn't as spectacular as I'd imagined. I guess I expected something miraculous by the way Jesus had been trying to get me to talk to him. But his story was simple, really.

His parents were people who pursued Jesus passionately and encouraged him to do the same. He hadn't gotten into any big trouble. Life just hadn't given him the opportunity to do so. He looked at me and said he didn't really understand why people responded to him in that way. But they did, and when they did, he simply praised Jesus for the opportunity to be something of a light in a person's life.

"Matthew," said the lead singer, seemingly exasperated because his bandmate wouldn't share too much. "This man spends time with Jesus. He prays. He makes an effort to know his Savior. His life is pure. He's not perfect or anything, but Jesus blesses that boy because he is faithful at spending time with Jesus. He knows him."

I liked the fact that someone else had to tell his story. The young man, who played bass and had fascinating hair, had a story that wasn't the least bit rehearsed. He seemed to be humble, a lot more humble than I am most of the time. Thankfully, I didn't walk away from that conversation feeling perverted, but I did leave asking Jesus to give me a little taste of what that bass player had. I walked away thinking I needed to readdress my own desire to really know Jesus. Knowing Jesus is of great importance to a pure heart.

I also left there thinking that the kind of pure heart Jesus talks about in Matthew 5 makes some pretty ordinary people quite magical.

heart

You're blessed when you get your inside world—your mind and heart—put right. Then you can see God in the outside world.

Matthew 5:8 The Message

I Had to Stop Running

I've heard many pastors, teachers, writers, singers, small group leaders, and regular people say a lot of *stuff* about what it means to have a pure heart. Most of them concentrate a lot of time on sexual purity. We Christians use words like *abstain* and *resist* and *run* when talking about sexual temptation. We use the words a lot.

I have grown tired of hearing these words as they relate to purity. It's not because I believe these actions of running and resisting aren't practical ways to avoid getting into "sexual" trouble once in a while. But honestly, resisting, abstaining, and running have never worked for me. Perhaps I am doing them wrong. Maybe I have the wrong kind of shoes or something. Maybe I don't have the right equipment to abstain. But I guess I've listened to an awful lot of men and women tell me running hasn't worked very well for them, either. I wish it did work. I wish the temptation to sin could be outrun. It would make my spiritual life a bit simpler, I believe.

While relearning Jesus, I've learned in order for my heart to be pure, whether from lust or pride or fear or unkindness or whatever I personally war against, it takes something very different than running and resisting. In fact, I learned the hard way that I can't run fast enough to keep my heart pure and escape sin. I'd constantly be running and getting absolutely nowhere. I used to run all the time. Sometimes I'm still tempted to run today. It's a part of my spiritual DNA to run. It's programmed inside of me somewhere.

I know and have spoken to so many people who are running now. When they tell me their stories, I see the look of frustration and tiredness in their eyes. Some of them are afraid to say their sin out loud. They give it to me in code. They're afraid I might judge them or think less of them because they just admitted to me they're addicted to pornography or unemotional sexual hookups or over-the-counter drugs or whatever else we humans get ourselves into. I know that feeling of fear, of saying it out loud. I've spoken to others in code before too.

Every one of these people asks me if I know a secret. They hope I have some kind of an answer they haven't learned yet. They're looking for an easy way (or just any way) out of their sin. They're looking to be suddenly fixed; they keep praying and hoping Jesus will come into their lives and miraculously remove the temptation from their lives. I know that look in their eyes because I've lived it. I still live it sometimes.

For me, it was almost as if temptation and I would play a game. As soon as I saw the temptation coming from a long way off, I'd put on my jogging shoes, I'd run as fast as I could, I'd say Bible verses, I'd take cold showers, I'd do push-ups, I'd think about butterflies, I'd call my accountability partner. I'd do anything to try and outrun temptation. Once in a while, I'd win a match or a race—and that would feel really good. But most of the time, temptation would outrun me—and then I'd lose. I'd lose because I was depending on my own ability, *thinking* I was depending on the power of Jesus in my life.

Sure, I've met men who are recovering sex addicts who wish they had run. In fact, one actually told me to "just run, man. You'll eventually find enough strength to run faster than temptation. It just happens, I promise."

I've also met women living in the aftermath of marriages destroyed by affairs who wish they or their husbands had resisted. The situations are devastating. So many have a battle strategy or a game plan, and I have tried them. The methods I've heard work for a while, but then it comes back on a day that I am tired or weak or frail (which is every day of my life, practically). And I lose—again.

But most of the time running and resisting don't work. I was devastated when I learned that my acts of resistance wouldn't (and couldn't) make my heart pure. It left me feeling empty and insecure in my faith.

I so wish I had a secret to share.

Only my time with Jesus has made purity of heart even an option for me. Traveling with Jesus on this journey continues to introduce me to the grace and forgiveness and purity that his blood supplies. When I finally decided to fall down and let Jesus pick me up, I began to slowly feel the nature of what grace is supposed to do for a person like me.

And after falling down more than a few times and letting Jesus continue to pick me back up out of my filth, I stopped running. I learned to accept his grace as a gift again and again. The gift is often hard to accept, I do admit.

Suddenly, it dawned on me I had been running nonstop for years. I tried outrunning lust. I tried outrunning bitterness. I tried outrunning pride. I tried outrunning fear. Everything my heart collected over the years, I tried to outrun. Basically, if it was a problem in my life, I just got prepared for a good game of tag. But it does suck when whatever it is that's chasing you says, "Tag, you're it." And that's happened more times than I can count.

Jesus has taught me to fall down a lot. Falling down and humbling myself in front of Jesus is usually when I see him. It's when my heart is at its purest—not perfect—just clean from confession and a little bit of humility. I still sometimes see things my eyes shouldn't see. I still hear things that my ears shouldn't hear, and sometimes I do things I don't want to do.

Yet it's my sincere desire to be completely dependent on Jesus. I want my life to hardly be able to function on its own. Jesus has to remind me my actions are selfish, that I'm completely useless without him on the journey. That's why I don't have a secret to share. If I did, it would mean I had *arrived* somewhere, and you might be tempted to look for that place too.

Today, when I feel the effects of temptation, when I can hear its footsteps running toward me, Jesus tells me not to run. He tells me to just fall down and resist depending on my own ability. When I do, sometimes when I finally stand up again, I have just enough strength to say no to whatever it is that is ailing me.

As you can imagine, I fall down on my face a lot.

But I've learned purity comes through humility. Purity can be seen over the horizon when my friend Daniel calls me up and asks me how I'm doing—*really* doing. Purity gives me a chance when I am weak enough to be completely honest with my friend. Purity comes when I know this story I am living is not about me. When I live out the truth that my story is about being a part of Jesus's story, purity of heart is a possibility.

I don't expect perfection anymore, but I do anticipate grace. I know that grace must be my lifeblood. Grace must be the thing that keeps me from running on my own strength. It takes a silly person to be pure. It might just take a personality as simple as my old co-worker Angela. Because I get a glimpse of God when I am foolish enough to simply follow Jesus as he leads me to invest my life into other people and not into myself.

That glimpse is magical, magical enough to encourage me to remain with Jesus on the journey. Today, I wake up most mornings desiring to see God do something through me or in front of me or despite me. I want that to be the desire of my heart. With that being my constant prayer, I know I cannot journey alone.

Purity of heart, for me, is all about dependency.

Happy to See You

Nicaragua in January is hot and muggy, much like a Houston summer. When we (a team of about twenty people) arrived at the airport in Managua in January 2003, two large white vans were there to pick us up and take us to the hotel.

I stared out the window in disbelief most of the way to our hotel. As we drove down the mostly dirt streets, we couldn't help but be physically and emotionally moved by the desperation and poverty that consumed the city. Everywhere I looked, I saw poor faces—hopeless, alone, fearful, dirty. The people looked like they had been locked up inside the jail of reality, and they couldn't find the key. In fact, most of them looked as if they had stopped looking. The look on their faces screamed, *We have no way of getting out.*

I was in Nicaragua with a large child relief organization. Upon arrival, I learned I might be able to meet Carlos, the child my wife and I sponsor. Three days later, I was told that Carlos would be at one of the camps that we would be visiting.

When I met eight-year-old Carlos, he was singing Jesus songs in his one-room schoolhouse with about seventy-five other poor children and a dedicated group of adult leaders. As we got out of the van, we could hear the children's praise spilling out into the very poor streets. One of the women who was with us, a thirty-something-year-old singer, looked at me upon hearing the sweet sound of music. "Do you hear that? That is one of the most beautiful sounds I have ever heard." She was right. The sound was about as close to magical as I had ever encountered. When I first heard the sound of those young Spanish-speaking voices singing out loud with their little hands clapping cheerfully, I couldn't believe my ears.

While the others continued to sing and clap, Carlos joined me out in the common area of the children's church and school. Their building was surrounded by some of the poorest neighborhoods I have witnessed. It appeared to be desolate for so many.

Carlos was quite tall for his age. His deep brown hair was sloppy and looked as if it hadn't been washed in a few days. He smelled of chocolate, thanks to a snack the children had just eaten. We chatted through an interpreter. Knowing that Carlos was only eight years old, I did my best to make my questions short, simple, and to the point. One of his answers to my silly questions left me speechless.

"Is there anything that you want, Carlos?" I asked, looking directly into his large brown eyes. "Is there anything, anything at all, that you *really* want?"

I watched as Carlos's glance turned to his interpreter and then listened intently to him as he translated my words. Carlos looked at me and shook his head.

"Nada," he said to the interpreter. *Nada* is one of the few words that I actually know in Spanish.

"Are you sure?" I asked again. "Do you want a TV? A soccer ball? Toys? Anything at all?"

Again, Carlos looked up at his interpreter and then responded again, "No, nada."

I asked the same question one more time, thinking to myself that there must be at least one selfish dream that this kid might have. This time Carlos thought about it for a moment. He turned to the interpreter and said shyly, "¿Puedo tener una cama a dormir encendido?"

"He wants a bed to sleep on," said the interpreter.

heart

He doesn't have a bed? He's poor enough to not have a bed, yet too shy and quiet and content to ask for one? And he refused to ask for anything remotely selfish?

I was speechless.

As I sat there and talked with Carlos, I couldn't help but be amazed at this kid's heart. He was happy. Even though he did not have a bed, it took him forever to think of something that he needed *or even wanted.* Despite his surroundings being so ugly and poor and, to an American like me, very much hopeless, Carlos and the other children and their noble leaders found reason and energy to praise Jesus.

I saw a vivid picture of Jesus that day, not in the clouds but on the face of Carlos and on the faces of the other children.

That night my heart was perplexed. I couldn't sleep. So, I walked around inside the comfort of the beautiful five-star hotel where I was staying, and I prayed this prayer:

Jesus, I feel guilt for seeing you in this moment, when it seems so gross and poor and poverty-stricken here. I feel like a stupid, proud American to even think about seeing you in such a place. It seems so very cliché. But the kids' hearts I witnessed today are so pure that they seem to be able to see you and praise you in spite of their circumstances. I believe with all of my heart that they see you. Would you please give me the freedom and purity to see you too? I want that.

Jesus showed up on several occasions over the next few days. I didn't make a big deal about it to the others when I saw him. I didn't jump up and down with excitement; I didn't have the energy, nor did I feel the need to point him out to everyone around.

In all honesty, I was just happy I was able to see him.

4

mercy

I have always found that mercy bears richer fruits
than strict justice.

Abraham Lincoln

The Hard Thing about Mercy

My friend Lisa, the intelligent Christian friend of mine who always got off on having long spiritual conversations, was driving to meet with a troubled teen from her youth group. On the ride over, she decided to call me for some much-needed encouragement.

As long as I have known Lisa, she has always put a great deal of effort into spending time with kids. But it's not just time she spends. She works hard at investing in the spiritual and emotional lives of the young girls in her youth ministry. She has seen a lot of sad things happen in her ministry time. If there is anyone in the world I know who understands the concept of how showing mercy often hurts like hell, it's her. She's learned this the hard way—by showing a lot of mercy.

"Hey, Mateo! Well, I'm on my way over to the juvenile detention center," said Lisa, in a sarcastic, singsong tone. *"Again!"*

"Which one of your kids has been sent there?" I asked.

"I probably shouldn't say," she replied. "You probably don't know her. This girl has stolen her parents' car two or three times since I've known her. And this is the first time her parents have actually allowed the police to arrest her. On top of that, she's tried to commit suicide before, and she's anorexic. Lucky me, huh?"

"Wow. I'm sorry to hear this," I said. "How *old* is she, Lisa?"

"She's fourteen," she said, softly. "And the thing is, Mateo, I have run out of things to say to this girl. I have spent I don't know how many hours of my youth ministry investing into her life . . . And you know me; I don't mind troubled kids. In fact, I *love* them. But I don't know what else to do for her. I feel helpless. So, I called you for some Mateo-support!"

"Has she ever improved?"

"Oh yeah, she does great for about two months. And then falls hard—and usually it's so much harder than before. She's probably going to get sent away to a girls' home. I'm scared for her, you know? I don't know if she will make it there."

"I don't know what to say, Lisa."

"I don't expect to hear any magic words."

"I know it's hard to give and give and give when nothing ever seems to change," I said. "That's the crazy thing about ministry, I guess; the 'return on investment' is not *really* the point. It's the fact that Jesus has asked us to give and give and give without expecting anything in return. I don't believe the lack of change should change our willingness to extend mercy."

"I know," said Lisa. "I just want this girl to see the dream God has for her, that's all. It *really* is hard to keep giving and giving and not see at least that. Do you know that I have been hanging out with her for more than a year and a half? And now, we're right back at the beginning."

"I actually doubt that's true, Lisa. This girl's circumstance may seem like she's back at the beginning, but she's probably not. I have little doubt that one of these days she'll look back on all of this and remember you."

"I'm not so sure," laughed Lisa.

"Oh, I think you'll be surprised. I think she'll one day look back on all of this time you've invested, and she'll see her need to make some changes."

"If she lives that long," said Lisa with a hint of seriousness in her voice. "Anyway, I am just emotionally wiped out from all of this. Would you please pray for me? I covet your prayers. It's just going to be hard to see her in jail."

Mercy is indeed hard.

Anytime I have ever seen the ongoing presence of mercy and compassion, there's always a time when the person doing the giving gets burned out. It's almost inevitable, I think.

The act itself—the emotional, spiritual, and physical investment—is sometimes just tiring. At times in my life when I'm brave enough to show mercy, there are moments when it feels like I've reached a dead end. I come expecting to find some kind of result. But instead I end up at a place that is nowhere close to my destination.

Everything inside says to give up. But that's hard, too, because mercy creates a bond. The connection Jesus forms between the giver and the recipient cannot simply be forgotten. Let me be truthful: too often I begin my ventures into showing mercy with an end—a good end—in mind. Whether it's for the recipient or me, I usually expect something miraculous to happen. When it doesn't turn out like we have prayed and hoped and imagined, discouragement too often abounds.

Jesus must have figured if he had let me in on how hard it is to show mercy and compassion without return, I would resist giving with all of my heart.

I once had the pleasure of hearing a wise man say this: To show mercy *once* is expected. To show mercy a *thousand times* is generous. To show mercy for a *lifetime* is to be the Savior of the world. So, let's always be generous.

Generous is beautiful but difficult.

I didn't always understand my part in mercy. I was once a bit stingy and selfish in my compassion and forgiveness. Sure, I gave of myself and my money when the moment was convenient. But the concept of mercy being a part of who I was as a person was quite foreign to me. Which is not surprising, considering I knew a lot more about the absence of mercy than I did about showing it.

On the journey, Jesus demands mercy of me.

An Unfortunate Tale

When I was in fifth grade I cheated on a math assignment. Well, I didn't *really* cheat on my math work. I still to this day believe it to be a complete misunderstanding. But to that year's grade school teacher, it was cheating to the worst degree.

Back then my school used a Christian education program called A.C.E. (Accelerated Christian Education). Despite its catchy name, A.C.E. might be one of the worst academic programs to ever exist. But I digress.

In this program, each year we were expected to complete twelve paces (thirty- to forty-page school booklets) in each subject. We worked at our own "pace." We even checked our own work at a "checking" table. It was at the checking table that I got into trouble.

One morning, after having been back and forth from my desk to the checking table exactly four times *and* still having only *one* of the thirty answers wrong, I copied that one answer from the grading book into my pace. So, technically, I *did* cheat. But really, I think if the teacher had given me a chance to explain the whole four times back and forth predicament, I think she would have understood. But like most scenarios in my school, it didn't work out that way.

Mrs. Bark caught me red-handed.

"Did I just see you copying an answer into your pace?" asked my fifth-grade schoolteacher.

I didn't know how to answer her question. Technically, I *had* just copied the answer from the grade book into my pace, but not *really*. It was quite confusing to me how I should address her concern. However, my silence didn't help my case much. She began to yell, as teachers in my school tended to do when they thought a student was disrespecting their authority.

"Go down to the principal's office!" yelled Mrs. Bark. As soon as she said those words, I froze at the thought of going to the principal. I wanted to stay there. Because Mrs. Bark's bite was certainly bad, but it was nothing like that of the principal who waited for me downstairs.

"But . . . I . . . didn't . . ."

"Do not say one more word to me, Matthew," bellowed Mrs. Bark. "Get downstairs immediately!"

"But, Mrs. Bark—"

"*Get downstairs! Go!* I do not want to hear another word."

If she had simply listened to my story, I think she would have understood. But her abrupt response surprised me, and I wasn't able to think fast enough for her.

I walked downstairs toward the principal's office. It felt like I was walking the longest plank that my mind could have imagined. Mercy was really hard to come by in *Mrs. Bark's class*. But I estimated, according to my limited amount of experience with the principal I was getting ready to meet with, that I would have had a better chance of being eaten by mad Chinese monkeys on my way to the office than to get shown any kind of mercy by the man behind the desk.

Just as I had expected, I received my first and only paddling that day (ten swaps with a wooden-holed paddle against my backside). There was *one* merciful thread in this story. *That* principal, after meeting the wrath of my mother, never touched me again—*ever!* A little vengeance toward a mean principal who wouldn't listen felt pretty merciful to me.

Unfortunately, this merci*less* experience was only one of many that I experienced growing up.

Harsh judgment rather than compassionate mercy seemed to rule in my church and school. I saw its ugly effects in the lives of my friends and acquaintances too many times to count. When I was in seventh grade, I watched as three tenth-grade boys got kicked out of my school and church for drinking beer. They hadn't gotten drunk; but they got caught. In tenth and then again in eleventh grade, the same expulsion took place with four girls who got pregnant. The judgment these individuals experienced didn't seem to contain even an ounce of mercy. You could feel the widespread sentiment throughout the school as word spread that another individual had just felt the sting of Christian wrath. Now I don't fault the church and school leadership for administering punishment. But without mercy, punishment is merely hatred with a point.

When mercy was void in those situations, so often the outcome had consequences too. After those three young men left church, they never engaged even *the idea* of Jesus again. One of them was killed in a motorcycle accident; he had been drinking. One became an alcoholic. Out of the four girls who had babies in high school, only one chases Jesus today. She began looking many years later for the father of the child she had in high school, but he had died suddenly in a tragic accident; he had gone to our school too. As for the other three pregnant girls, they have always just seemed to exist without passion, without peace, and without anything *real* to hold onto.

I don't believe my church necessarily *caused* these problems. People certainly make poor choices and must learn to live with the consequences. But I do believe one or two acts of mercy could have *changed* these people's outcomes. Because mercy tends to do that; it changes things.

Because those seven individuals received and developed very merciless perspectives of Jesus, they chose to walk away from experiencing him altogether. It's been my life experience that in the absence of mercy, more pain and tragedy is inevitable. However, I've learned the *hard way* (as with most things in this book) that showing mercy doesn't guarantee happiness and healing. Nonetheless, it's our calling; it's expected of us.

Mercy Shouldn't Have Stipulations

As clumsy as showing mercy feels sometimes, I always believe in it.

James was prone to making stupid mistakes. He made a lot of them. If it wasn't his sleeping around (or trying to) that got him into trouble, it was driving 95 in a 40, underage drinking, and hanging out with the crowd that did all of the above and then some. Unfortunately for him, James had the luck of post-1992 Michael Jackson. Except if James were caught with his pants down (and one time that actually happened), punishment usually followed.

When I moved to Northern Virginia, seventeen-year-old James began working for me at the coffeehouse/live-music venue I managed. Over time, we developed the kind of relationship that allowed me to be the one "adult" he would sometimes listen to. As I got to know James, he began to open up more. We developed a great deal of trust between us. Because our religious pasts were similar, I chose not to "preach" at him *too* much. Rather than harping on him about his smoking and drinking habits, I chose to make sure he felt mercy from at least one individual in his life. But over those two years of working alongside James, I wondered a million times if I was doing the right thing. Because it was one of the hardest things I have ever been able to do.

One night about an hour before James's midnight shift was to be over, he and two of his buddies were out behind the coffeehouse. With two bags of trash in my hand, I walked out the back door toward the dumpster only to find James and his crew smoking marijuana. He was holding a partly empty bottle of vodka. Upon seeing this sight, I cursed and dropped the trash bags.

"Please, get inside, James!" I said as controlled as I possibly could.

As soon as those words bellowed out of my mouth, I'm sure it will come as no surprise that my mind started thinking a thousand thoughts: *This is the third time he's done something like this. Do I call his parents this time? Do I ruin the trust that we have built? Do I tell him the same stuff he's heard a million times? How does mercy fit in to all of this?*

Once the back door slammed behind us, James spoke first.

"I am so sorry that I'm putting you in another predicament you don't want to be in, Matthew," he said. "I won't let this happen again."

"You've done this before," I said, still trying to figure out what I was going to do.

"I know, bro. I am so sorry."

"I'm sure you are, James," I said, giving way to a subtle laugh. "I'd feel sorry, too, if I was a seventeen-year-old who had just gotten caught smoking pot and hitting shots at work—*again.*"

"What are you going to do?" he asked.

I didn't answer his question.

"You *promised* the last time that you would *never* put me in this position again," I said. "I *hate* this, James. This just isn't fair."

"I know," he whispered.

Two minutes went by without either of us saying a word to each other. I prayed inside my head. I'm quite sure James was praying too. My words broke the silence.

"Get out of here, bro," I said.

When he heard those words, James's face went from desperate to confused.

"As long as you're OK to drive, then get out of here," I said.

"That's it? No lecture? You're not going to at least give me the same talk you did the last time?"

"No, I'm not," I said. "It just dawned on me, James, I've shown you *my* mercy the last two times: I let you go but then made you promise me that you'd never do it again. But I'm realizing that's kind of like showing mercy and then attaching a bomb to it."

James stared at me intently.

"The kind of mercy Jesus shows is limitless. It doesn't come with stipulations. Besides, I don't want you promising me something you can't deliver. You don't have to promise me anything, James. I forgive you. This little event will stay between you and me. Now, get out of here. You've got to work tomorrow morning."

"Are you sure?"

"Yes, I'm sure. Go."

"Thanks, Matthew," he said, "I promise . . ."

"*Don't do it*, James. Don't promise something you aren't able to keep. Just accept the gift."

James gathered his stuff and headed for the door. As he walked away, I thought of so many things I wanted to say. I wanted to remind him drug abuse has consequences that might not be nearly as merciful. I wanted to tell him not to forget this moment, to remember it when he was feeling like mercy didn't exist. I wanted to tell him not to take mercy for granted, but then thought of how many times I had taken it for granted. So, as James said good-bye one last time before heading out the front door, I wanted to say a lot of things, but I kept my mouth closed—for once.

Nearly five years later, out of the blue, I got an e-mail from James. He had just started going back to church. Just two years before he had gotten busted for possession. But a good lawyer got him out of it. Obviously, he later learned that drugs have *some* consequences. In his e-mail he also wrote, "I just wanted to thank you for showing me a kind side of Jesus; I had never met that side of him before. I'm back in church exploring my faith again."

For me, that letter was magical.

I've shared that story only once in front of an audience. After I finished my talk, several people came up to me afterward and said that they thought my decision to not report him was atrocious. When I asked them why, they said things like, "You could have kept him from getting arrested. He might not have ever done drugs again. Mercy could have come in the form of his parents getting involved." They were right; mercy could have come in all of those forms. But at the time I made that decision, I didn't care about the pot. I didn't care about the vodka. I was more concerned about him experiencing a small—*very small*—taste of mercy, forgiveness, and grace.

> You're blessed when you care. At the moment of being "carefull," you find yourselves cared for.
>
> Matthew 5:7 The Message

Shock

If the *mercy of Jesus* shocks me, why shouldn't the mercy I show to others be shocking too? Jesus's mercy doesn't *make sense*. It's alarming and peculiar. It gives and gives and gives without expecting anything from me in return. The mercy of Jesus catches me off guard at times. I believe that's the most effective kind of mercy in this world—the kind that leaves me standing back and wondering what just happened. That's the kind of mercy that changes people's lives. That's the kind of mercy I need in my own life—the kind of mercy which leaves me amazed and in disbelief.

Jesus talked about mercy like this: the one who shows mercy is happy because he is shown mercy. The times in my life I have been shown mercy are memorable, peaceful, and spiritual. It's like being reintroduced to Jesus all over again. Mercy makes me think to myself, *Ah, this is what Jesus is supposed to feel like.*

But revealing that kind of mercy takes a selfless person. I know exactly what mercy looks like and, still, I fail to show it often enough. Sure, it's pretty simple for me to show mercy in a situation like James's. It's just me showing forgiveness. It hardly takes any action at all. Certainly that kind of mercy isn't *always* easy, but in many cases it is indeed easy.

For me, the hard-to-show mercy is the intentional kind of mercy I am called to hand out daily and willingly in the lives of those in need, in want, or in pain. That kind of mercy actually takes time, effort, energy, and finances on my part. On the journey, Jesus has really been teaching he simply wants mercy to be a part of my lifestyle—in that it becomes natural, an obsession perhaps, for me to give of myself freely and openly in someone's life.

In the past, I thought I lived this way a few times.

Sure, I've fed the homeless on Thanksgiving and New Year's Day. I support a child with Compassion International and another with World Vision. I give money when disasters hit. I put coins in the red Salvation Army cans at Christmas. I give my leftover clothes and house items to people in need. But does any of this really cost me all that much? And isn't mercy something that is free but costs a lot?

My friend Eileen believes so. She believes it with all of her heart.

Another Person's Thoughts on the Subject

I shared part of Eileen's story in my book *Provocative Faith*. She was the brave woman who forged past the skepticism and negativity of closed-minded Christian men and finally got to Jerusalem as a missionary. Today, Eileen lives in a two-room flat on the east side of the Holy City. She works with Hebrew youth and young adults. Her work has helped develop Jesus-centered mission camps all over Israel. In the winter, she translates Christian information into Hebrew. However, before all of that, Eileen learned from her mother and father how to celebrate Jesus through mercy.

"People have always raised their eyebrows at what my family and I have done," wrote Eileen. "I stopped long ago caring what others think. I'm not serving them. Mercy knows no boundaries in my opinion."

Eileen's stories and rousing spirit often left me feeling affected in my faith. I wanted Eileen's passion about mercy to be shared. So, I asked her a few questions about Jesus, mercy, and receiving mercy. Some of her answers are a little out of the ordinary. But shouldn't I have expected as much from a fifty-eight-year-old woman who enjoys a little tequila with her vanilla ice cream?

Matthew: Eileen, what is your first memory of feeling mercy?

Eileen: My mother was full of compassion, love, and mercy. As you know, I grew up in a small town in the southern part of Alabama. That little town was 50 percent white and 50 percent black. And very much divided. My family had very little growing up. But that didn't stop my mom from giving. When I was four years old, we would get up very early in the morning on Mondays, Wednesdays, and Fridays. We drove about fifteen miles to the other side of the town, and we'd deliver fruits, vegetables, breads, and canned goods to the poor people. We had a big garden, and that was my mom's way of giving back. Mom would often help them with their finances, balance their checkbooks, and even give them tips on raising children. Those have to be my earliest memories. Even though I wasn't the recipient of the mercy, I certainly felt it.

Matthew: Your mom became quite a controversy at times in your little town, didn't she?

Eileen: (Laughs.) That's an understatement. My mom caused quite a stir. The town we lived in was still very racist back then. Many of the folks Mom helped—not all but most—were people of color. Lots of people, even the church people, didn't like that my mom associated herself with black people. We'd get letters in the mail calling my mom and dad "nigger lovers." It was scary at times. But my mom never let that influence what she did. She certainly feared for my safety a couple of times, but then she'd pray the protection of Jesus over me and move on.

Matthew: What did your father think about all of this?

Eileen: Well, Daddy was a giver in his own right. On Saturdays, he'd convert our garage into a place where poor people could come and get their cars worked on. Nearly *every* Saturday from nine to three, Daddy would work on cars. Which really, caused more of a controversy than Mom's good deeds, because it meant black people were coming over to the "white" side of town. I remember one occasion when I was about eight or nine, Daddy saw a man pull into our driveway. He knew he had come to cause trouble. Daddy yelled, "Leeny,"—that's what he called me—"get in the house, girl." I ran into the house and then watched the scene from my bedroom window. The man was drunk and cursing and screaming, calling my dad all sorts of names, but Dad was just as patient with him as he was with the poor people. He didn't see any difference. He used to say that people like that were "needy" too. "Just needy in a different way."

Matthew: Where do you believe your parents got this innate desire to give of their lives?

Eileen: It was certainly a product of their faith. But it wasn't a faith they found at church on Sunday. It was the faith in Jesus they had learned from living life. Each of them found Jesus's words about the poor and needy and sick to be *real*. So, instead of making lots of money, they really concentrated on investing it into people. I always laugh when I think about this, but I pretty much watched most of my inheritance get given away to people every day of my life. And I think about that now and am blown away by how special a gift that was to me.

Matthew: How did your mom and dad's way of life influence your own life?

Eileen: I think when you have parents like I had, you can either run far away from that kind of lifestyle or you embrace it fully. I know people who grew up in homes like mine, and those people are now extremely bitter about what their parents put them through—the ridicule and all. But I embraced it. I got teased a little when I was in high school, but it wasn't about my hair or my clothes or my weight—it was because my parents were being nice to people. How can I really be upset about that? My parents walked the narrow road. They taught me what it meant to be the salt of the earth. And surprise, surprise, Matthew! It had nothing to do with being at church every Sunday or singing good songs or reading the right books. It had nothing to do with Bible studies and choir practice and Sunday school. It had nothing to do with sermons and all the other stuff Christians find so much delight in. It's about giving my life away for nothing in return.

Matthew: You bring up an interesting point. I think a lot of people show mercy to get something back. What are your thoughts about that?

Eileen: It's preposterous to look at mercy as a way of *investing*.

Matthew: Oh, really? I use that term in my book. Why is that a bad term?

beatitude

Eileen: It's not a *bad* term necessarily. But the word *investing* implies you're going to get something back for what you do. It implies when you show mercy and compassion and forgiveness, you're looking for the recipient to all of a sudden be financially stable like you. Or smart like you. Or not on drugs like you. Or hope-filled like you. Showing mercy is not about the *return*, Matthew. It's about us giving—giving freely, often, and now. My parents once in a while saw some of the people who they helped get to a place where they didn't need help any longer. I've seen that in my work too. But if you're walking into a mercy experience and you're expecting your *investment* to turn a life around or make a poor person's life immaculate and perfect, you're showing mercy for the wrong reason. The *only* thing we should expect from showing mercy *is to be shown mercy*. Does mercy change lives? Yes! All the time. But if you expect it, you're going to get discouraged. You're going to get burned out. You're going to feel overwhelmed. Jesus just said give. He didn't put any stipulations on it. That wasn't his message.

Matthew: So, for you, what has been the most rewarding part of pursuing a life of mercy?

Eileen: There have been so many reasons. It's hard to say just one. I'll tell you this story: About a year and a half ago, I was here in Jerusalem, working at one of the Christian camps about an hour south of the city. I met a twelve-year-old girl named Sara. She had been rescued out of sexual slavery. Nobody knew where this little girl lived. Nobody knew her history. The pain she had experienced had caused her to go silent; she wasn't talking at all. To look at her sad face made my heart break. She was sent to the camp because the local police knew I had a little background in sexual abuse counseling. That is a miraculous story all its own, but *I knew* Jesus had sent this little girl to the camp because he loved her. I ended up letting her live with me (again, another miracle that is hardly ever allowed).

Over the course of the next few months, I basically kept her around me the entire time. I fed her. I let her sleep in my bed while I slept on the couch. I let her come to work with me. I tried to show her love. My mission board got her medical help. Two and a half months went by, and she was still not talking. One night, we were both at home. She was coloring. I was watching TV. Out of nowhere came this little voice: "Eileen." I didn't make a big deal about it. I answered her like we spoke to each other all of the time. But inside, I am *dancing.* "Do you think God loved me?" She *asked* me that question. I was thinking, *Thank you, Jesus!* We talked for three hours. We talked about her mom and dad, who we eventually were able to locate. We talked about her faith. We talked about what had happened to her.

Now fast-forward this story by about nine months. She's home. She's getting the counseling she needs. She's rediscovering life again. Me, on the other hand, I am feeling depressed, alone, and very much in a spot where I didn't think I could go on in ministry. I prayed to God, *Please, show me your vision for me. I just need to know you're alive.* Matthew, that's all I prayed. About fifteen minutes later, the phone rang. It was Sara. She just called to talk to me. We had only spoken once since her return home, and that was a week after she had left my home. I thought it would be good for her to get back to a normal routine and life. But when I heard her voice on the phone that night, I knew immediately that it was God giving me a taste of his mercy. It was him reminding me of his vision for me.

Matthew: One more question: Why do you believe we struggle to show mercy the way Jesus intended?

Eileen: I think it's simple and complicated all at the same time. We *think* we're *sold-out* for Jesus. I hear people tell me that all the time. But really, Matthew, do we even know what that means anymore? To some that means going to every church thing possible. And that's fine. But is that really the mission of Jesus—for us to be gathered around each other reading our Bibles like good little Christians? *Most of us know what Scripture teaches.* Go out and *live* it. I have a friend who lives in Maryland who twice a week gets up in the morning and drives elderly people to their doctors' appointments. I know a man in Sacramento who has a full-time job as a lawyer, but manages to volunteer *twenty* hours a week at a kids' hospital. *That's* being sold-out for Jesus. Even though my friends would probably never use that terminology. Our priorities are screwed up, Matthew. We've got our eyes on the wrong things. We wouldn't know mercy if it bit us in the rear. I give full-time because that is what I am called to do. *Everybody* can't do that. But everybody can look for some way to *invest* in the lives of people. Mercy is needed *everywhere*.

Relearning Jesus, Relearning Mercy

Valerie, a friend of mine in Nashville, is very honest about life. Having been raised in a Christian home since birth, she has seen a lot of the ins and outs of the conservative Christian faith. Her story isn't necessarily a new one. She's simply one of thousands, perhaps millions, of Christians who are somewhat disillusioned by their spiritual past.

Consequently, Valerie seeks more out of life than simply what the church often preaches. She admits to being bitter at times, even cynical. She's worked in Christian entertainment for many years. In her work, Valerie's had a bird's-eye view of what seemingly is wrong about pop-cultural Christianity. Of course, Valerie acknowledges the good too. But that's sometimes harder for her to see. The politics and business of all things Christian can dim the "light" for her a bit.

But I find her friendship to be like a circus in the midst of ten funerals. She's lively and humorous. Her cynicism is sometimes simply delightful. Sure, she surprises me with some of the things that come out of her mouth. "I *hate* praise and worship music," she told me once with utter sarcasm. Inside, I was tempted to think, *Can you be a Christian and hate "Here I Am to Worship"?*

However, at the same time, Valerie surprises me with some of the things that come out of her life too. Despite where Valerie is in the specifics of her Christian faith, her mercy toward people challenges me. The way she lives life, for me, has been quite convicting. It's shocking; it's the kind of relentless mercy that leaves those much more rigid and defined in their faith to scratch their heads and question their intentions. But that would only happen if they knew the *real* Valerie—the nonprofessional side of her doesn't get broadcast to everyone around. She keeps it quiet, except to her closest friends.

Everything about Valerie is big. Her personality. Her stories. Even her hair at times can take on a rather larger-than-life existence. Valerie and I have lunch once a month. My wife jokes about her being "the other woman" in my life. Every time Valerie and I get together, she leaves me wanting to be a little more like

Jesus (and, of course, she also provides a little comic relief). At lunch last year, she told me about something new going on in her life.

"So, have I told you what's going on in my life of late?" she asked loudly and as soon as we had sat down for lunch one afternoon.

"No, I guess not," I replied. I was expecting to hear a story about her work or kids.

"I am *donating* my bone marrow," she said, with a hilarious look that basically said "I have no idea what I am getting myself into."

"*You're what?!*" I said, completely shocked. "Does someone in your family have cancer?"

"Nope. Not like that at all. I was just thinking one day that I have all of this perfectly good bone marrow in my body; why not share it? So, I put myself on the list."

I laughed.

"Wow. Valerie, that *is* brave. Will it hurt?"

"Yep, like a muuutha."

"So, when do you go through with it?"

"That's the thing; I signed up for this *months* ago. Out of the blue, they called me last week. It could not have come at a worse time. But what are you going to do, say no to a man who is dying of cancer? So, I cleared my schedule . . . going into surgery next week."

"That's unbelievable; I'm proud of you."

"Why? I would hope someone would do the same thing for me," said Valerie. "But I got to tell you, it's much more of a process than I expected. I have to have blood exams; I'm going to be out of work for a while. It's *huge*."

"Do you get to meet the person you're donating to?"

"No. I don't know him. He doesn't know me. It will stay that way."

"That's crazy, Valerie. I'm excited for you. At least, I think I am."

Actually, I shouldn't have been surprised. Valerie does this kind of stuff all the time. She regularly volunteers her time to rock crying AIDS babies at a local hospital. She takes her daughters and their friends on surprise weekend getaways. She was one of the first people in line when a church bus headed south to Mississippi to help clean up after Hurricane Katrina. She has opened her home to strangers. She helps her friends when they are in need. Her life makes me feel stupid and selfish.

So what if she stands outside of the church on Sunday mornings until the praise and worship music is over? Who cares? She gives away a lot more worship to Jesus through how she lives than I do when I'm singing for thirteen minutes with my arms half-raised on Sunday morning.

I am learning mercy. When someone does me wrong and asks for forgiveness, I try to be quick to comply. But when it comes to offering mercy to strangers who do not ask, I am still in the process of letting mercy be a part of who I am.

Over these many years of being Christian, I have often asked Jesus for mercy.

I've also asked him many times where I can show mercy.

It's in his answer to the second question I find my answer to the first.

5

truth

The truth shall make you free.

Truth Hurts

While sitting at Caffeine, a Nashville coffeehouse, two men at a table next to me were talking—*loudly*. One of the guys, who was in his mid- to late twenties, was obviously a Christian. At first, I only assumed this because he was carrying a Bible with him. Later on, I got the Christian vibe from the guy's conversation. The other guy seemed to be your average college-jock-turned-insurance-salesman. I figured the twenty-eight-year-old (he said his age) had been a college guy only interested in beer and sex. Now that he was out of college, I was pretty sure he was interested in money too.

In the course of ten minutes, those two colleagues covered everything from politics to Jessica Simpson to Africa's AIDS problem. When they began talking about the jock's marriage woes, I *really* began listening.

"Hey, just because I am a married man doesn't mean I can't do a little sightseeing once in a while," said the jock loud enough for me to hear him. "You know what I mean? That chick behind the counter is a looker, huh?"

The Christian's rebuttal was frank and honest.

"Now, *you know* if your wife were to hear you say that, she'd be hurt, bro," he replied very kindly. "I don't think you should talk like that."

The jock replied slowly.

"What she don't know won't hurt her, man. You know what I mean?"

The jock had an obnoxious habit of always saying "you know what I mean?" after every one of his sentences. It seemed like a nervous habit of some sort.

"I *don't* know what you mean," said Christian. "I think you need to respect your wife, whether she's here or not. I think it's disrespectful for you not to."

"Hey, *Jesus*, I don't want to hear your sermon," said Jock somewhat seriously. "You know what I mean? Just keep your preaching to yourself. If I want your opinion, I'll be the first to ask for it. Until then, shut the h—— up."

Wow. This is getting kind of intense between them, and awkward for me.

Christian's face turned a couple shades of red because he knew that Jock's voice was carrying through the coffeehouse. So, Christian leaned in close and spoke in a loud whisper. I had to work at it, but I could still hear.

"You know what your problem is? You hate the truth."

"What is that supposed to mean? What do you mean, I *hate* the truth?" asked Jock.

"Whenever someone tells you the truth about yourself, you get uncomfortable and defensive. I've worked with you now for two years and you've never been able to handle truth. *Never.*"

After nearly five minutes of silence, the two of them picked up their briefcases, threw away their coffee cups, and headed for the door. On the way out Jock spoke up; he had obviously been thinking a lot about what Christian had said.

"You know what I think? I think you know as much truth about me as I do about your sex life. Oh wait; you don't *have* a sex life, do you?"

As the two left, the *looker* behind the counter peeked over at me, obviously having heard the conversation.

"I guess the *truth* hurts, huh?" she commented.

Then she laughed.

Before the Journey with Jesus Ever Began

My third semester at Belmont University was actually the beginning of my fourth year of college. Being that Belmont had some lingering Christian roots, many students attended because it offered the potential for a faith community. I had come the year before with that mindset too. I decided on Belmont because of its music business program, but also because I believed it would be a place, unlike my time at the community college, where my "faith foundation" would be strengthened and not challenged.

About a month into my fourth year, a new friend invited me to attend a local church's Bible study that he had been attending for a while. Excited about the potential for Christian growth, I jumped at the chance to be spiritually fed.

When we arrived, I found my place among the other clean-faced Jesus lovers. We sang songs, we ate food, and we fellowshiped. It was pretty much like any other Christian Bible study I had attended the year before.

As Kirk, the speaker with a serious mullet, was giving his talk, he really quite impressed me at first with his knowledge of Scripture.

Not too many people were spiritually impressive to me. Back then, I was quite confident in my biblical expertise, but Kirk seemed to be on an entirely different level. Of course, there might have been one small difference between him and me: I didn't necessarily know the Bible because I had fallen in *love* with the Word of God; I had just simply been fed Scripture and Bible stories all my life. Kirk seemed impassioned by the Word of God. Not only did he seem to know it, but he also seemed to love it.

As Kirk spoke, I simply listened and agreed with all that he said. I advertised my agreement with an occasional knowing nod and a soft but firm "uh huh." While others seemed to be eating up his knowledge of truth like they had been starving for weeks, I was sitting there thinking, *You didn't know this stuff? Gosh, I learned that when I was, like, ten.*

"Guys, here's the thing," preached Kirk passionately. "We did not choose God; God chose each one of us. Salvation through his blood was not a choice for you."

Suddenly, out of nowhere, I witnessed Kirk's little message about the love of God take what I thought then to be a doctrinal nosedive into the depths of "Reformed" deceit.

Did I just hear him correctly?

My ears perked up when he said those words. I sat there thoroughly convinced I must have heard him wrong. He couldn't have said any such thing.

"You would not be here this evening pursuing Jesus if it weren't for him having already known your name long before this earth was ever made. He *predestined* you to be a part of the kingdom. It's not by anything you did; it's all about him and what he did. In other words, he chose you."

What the . . . ?!

The heresy alert siren went off in my head. In my mind, the

words "false prophet" blinked like a flashing road sign. *What is all this predestination talk about?*

Sure, I was a recovering fundamentalist Baptist, but at the time, I was certainly not ready to hand over my theology to some educated Reformed punk who thought God was sending people to hell. I knew very little about predestination, but I knew it was not what I believed. Truthfully, I had only heard the word *predestination* once before, and it was from a preacher who my church called a Calvinist. When I was a teenager, I didn't know what being a Calvinist meant. But to anyone in my old church, if you were to admit that you were a Calvinist, it was the same as confessing you were—*God forbid!*—a Catholic. My old church gave Calvinists and Catholics the same "you poor thing" look of awful distress.

I just watched in horror as Kirk continued talking.

"And when Jesus chose you to be his kid, you escaped the flames of hell because he loved you that much," continued Kirk. "We are depraved human beings who cannot do one good thing unless the Father deems it so. Who are we to think that we can choose God . . ."

As I sat there, irritated by his message and shaking at the thought of all these uninformed Christians having no clue that what Kirk was speaking about was heresy, I had no idea what I was going do.

Should I raise my hand and say something?

That seemed like a pretty good idea at the time. So, I raised my hand.

"Umm, do you have a comment?" Kirk asked.

"What is your response to the verse, 'Whosoever shall call upon the name of the Lord will be saved'? *Who-so-ever!* That's in the Bible. Jesus said that."

At the sound of my voice, every eye in the room looked at me. Suddenly, I felt like a kid who had just kicked the soccer ball into his own team's goal. I know that feeling well because I was that kid on many occasions.

"I'm sorry, but what's your name?" Kirk asked, looking completely shocked by my question.

I have him on the run. He doesn't know what to say to me.

"My name is Matthew."

"Well, Matthew, most of the people in this room believe that 'no one comes to *Me* unless the Father draws him.' That's also in the Bible. In fact, Jesus said that too."

He is being sarcastic.

As I spoke to Kirk, I could sense how uncomfortable everyone else in the room was feeling because of this conversation. But I continued because I thought it was very important. By that time, I was getting pretty emotional.

"But what about free will?" I countered. "The idea that God gives us the freedom to make a choice."

"Free will is pretty much a myth," said Kirk.

"A myth? You think it's a myth? So, you're saying to me you believe God sends people to hell because he does not choose them?"

"I didn't say that. Man's sin sends us to hell; God simply doesn't choose every person."

"How is that hopeful?" I asked. "This is the most unbelievable thing I have ever heard. Jesus said that 'whosoever shall call upon the name of the Lord shall be saved.' And you're saying something completely opposite of that."

"Well, I don't think I should discuss this with you in front of an entire room of people who believe this way. If you want to continue this discussion, why don't we do it afterward?"

The friend who had invited me could tell I was very emotional. He put his arm around my shoulder and said, "Dude, chill, bro."

I tried to chill, but all I really did was shut up. Kirk went back to talking, while I sat there listening to what I thought was perverted lies. I was fuming inside. I had never heard such a ridiculous theory in all my life. *God sends people to hell? He chooses us? The blood of Jesus is limited?*

As the thought of such a series of events filled my mind, I could feel tears building in my eyes. I knew if I didn't get out of that room quickly, I would soon be crying. I took a couple of deep breaths and then I quietly walked toward the bathroom. As I walked past them, people whispered. Kirk stumbled over a word. That made other people look. One guy snickered. My friend was embarrassed. I felt like an idiot.

Once I got to the bathroom, I felt like I was close to hyperventilating. I couldn't breathe. So, I began praying. *God, what is this? Do you really send people to hell? I can't believe that. I don't believe that. This can't be truth.*

A Virgin Doubter

My version of "truth" has made me do some crazy things over the years. But the me who rallied against Reformed thinking back then was doing exactly what I would do when I was a twenty-year-old college student. When it came to the things of God, I believed I knew it all. When I believed in something, *really* believed, it came naturally for me to do whatever necessary to protect, honor, and proclaim that belief. That fervor was just a part of my human spirit. I can still be that passionate from time to time, especially if it's about something I indeed love or believe in.

I'm still a passionate person, but I'm much more controlled today than when I was twenty. And it's not just in my faith that I get passionate but also in marriage, family, pop culture, love, and politics. I don't like sitting back and watching life go by me; I want to involve myself in the process. But sometimes my passion to engage in the process gets me into some serious trouble.

That experience with Kirk and his "Reformers" at the conservative Presbyterian Bible study turned out to be quite influential in my spiritual life. Before that day, I had never once questioned what I believed to be true. Sure, I had questioned the rules, but not the doctrine. Sure, I thought the church's lack of love was ridiculous, but they were still, in my mind, biblically sound.

Up until that day, whatever I had been told by my pastor, Sunday school teachers, and high school teachers, I took as truth. My doctrine had never been challenged, and I liked it that way. When I was twenty, I didn't even know how important (or non-important) doctrine was to my Christian faith. I had always been taught that it was *quite* important. So, I held it in high esteem. But I didn't *really* know. I only knew what I believed to be true.

After meeting a roomful of people who seemed to believe a very different version of the Jesus story than I had been taught, I started asking questions. To a legalist, questions weren't a good thing.

At first, I really just wanted to know about predestination and Calvinism. So, my questions were rather simple at the beginning. But as I began to dig deeper into my personal beliefs and compare them to Scripture, I realized certain parts of my fundamentalist background didn't hold much spiritual water. I had always hated the legalism part of where I came from, but I had never thought to question or challenge or contradict what my church had been selling me as biblical truth.

But just because I had questions, that certainly didn't mean I simply jumped from one doctrinal belief to another. Because of the questions I had about my own church's doctrine, I didn't want to cling to somebody else's version of truth. I was afraid I would find out that it was wrong too. A small part of me felt like my church must have been in the middle of a grand conspiracy to keep the truth from regulars like me. Sure, it sounds crazy now, but to me, back then, it felt like I was in the middle of a *DaVinci Code*–style plotline, and I was the protagonist who was called to save the day.

OK, so I didn't end up saving much of anything, but in light of my predicament, I decided I needed a good boxing match with God. But because I was unprepared to box God—not that you can ever *really* be prepared for such an event—my God-match ended up resulting in a lot more questions than answers.

When I had finally finished asking questions, I ended up doubting Jesus and becoming confused about whether or not there was reality of truth. In the early fall of 1994, for the first time in my life, I was at a place of doubt. That moment was gut wrenching; it felt as though everything in my heart and soul had been turned into a code I couldn't decipher. I was spiritually lost. Sadly, nobody *really* knew it, or if they did, they didn't tell me they knew it.

I had only read about doubt a few times in a "liberal" Christian magazine. I was afraid to doubt, but eventually it was all I had to lean on. From the day I realized I could poke holes in some of the basic theology of my church, truth didn't make much sense.

This Is My Life, Starring Doubt

I so wish doubt were a place—like a retreat center where addicts go to find rehab or therapy. It would be great to have a place where, whenever you felt doubtful about Jesus, you could simply check yourself into the facility. If doubt were a destination, life would be easier. It would have been much simpler to experience if I had been guaranteed that six to eight weeks later someone smarter than I would label me "Christian" again.

But I found out quickly doubt wasn't a place. Doubt ended up being more like a companion to me. Just one day out of the blue, doubt suddenly popped into my life unannounced. Like an annoying great aunt that I tried desperately to entertain, doubt would show up and stay for a week or two.

During those times when doubt drove with me on my journey, I felt as though everything I knew to be true broke down around me. Sure, I still went through the motions of church, but I fought against feeling anything. At that time in my life, my friendship with doubt had become borderline codependent. I clung to her side when my doctrine and theology didn't make much sense. She was my bucket whenever my spirituality sprang a leak. It was easier to hang with doubt than to find faith or truth. Faith and truth were like strangers to me when doubt was around.

However, despite having moments of severe doubt, my big questions never led me to lose my faith in God completely. It's not like I became atheist or agnostic overnight. Sure, some people certainly go to that extreme. But for me, doubt made me feel like I was simply hanging in the balance between what I believed to be true and what was actually happening in my life. Doubt often made me feel ready to throw in the spiritual towel. The truth that doubt existed inside of me was overwhelming because I had been told early on in my faith to fear anything which remotely resembled doubt.

In the midnineties, doubt was not popular in Christian circles— at least not like it is today. Churches back then were still getting used to not using hymnals every Sunday; I knew they wouldn't understand a little healthy doubt. And in fact, as far as I was concerned, I couldn't tell anyone what I was experiencing; it would have been considered sin by most—at least, most people I knew.

The very *idea* of spiritual doubt—including questions about Jesus, the virgin birth, the resurrection, and other such Christian standards—was preposterous. I looked, but I found very few books on the subject. However, I didn't look too hard. It always felt like I disowned my faith when I went to *that* part of the bookstore.

Pastors rarely mentioned it from behind their pulpits. No authors rambled poetically about their evangelical frustrations—not like they do now. A few musicians certainly tried to bring some light to the subject of Christian doubt, but their songs were never played—not on the radio anyway.

Today, things seem to be different. There seems to be a place for a little reasonable doubt within the church walls. Now seemingly open to at least hearing and considering the "postmodern" voice, some churches even celebrate the fact that doubt exists in the church. A few well-known, nonreligious books give passion to that voice. Where once you could only find books full of heavy-handed advice, spiritual inspiration, and virginity methods, you now find bookstores open to the idea that not everyone in the church can (or even cares to) relate to James Dobson or Pat Robertson.

However, before 1994, doubt had never been a part of my vocabulary. Even if I had felt its nasty tentacles wrapping their way around my heart and mind, I certainly would have *never* told anyone. But despite the need to keep it on the down-low, I doubted; I simply refrained from talking about it. It was kind of like the old "don't ask, don't tell" policy for gays and lesbians in the military. Churches knew doubters existed in their congregations, but most of them didn't want to know them by name. Some churches still adhere to this kind of thinking.

The first friend I spoke to about my doubt said, "What? You're a Christian; what is there to possibly doubt?"

"I don't know," I replied. "I'm just not sure about where Jesus fits into my life anymore."

"Come on, man," he said. "You don't want to go to hell. What if Jesus came back tonight and caught you doubting? Don't you think he would be kind of upset with you? You might not even make it into heaven, bro."

For a moment, my friend's words tempted me to feel guilty and confess, but my passion to figure out what the heck Jesus was all about helped me refrain. My friend didn't seem to understand. I guess it was because he wasn't in my shoes. But really, how could I have expected him to be OK with my doubt? His best friend had just blurted out he doubted the very thing that was supposed to be the center of his life. Today, I think fondly of my friend's concern. Sure, he made some stupid comments, but I love that he cared enough to say something to me.

When I walked through this, I found it funny how people would react to me when I told them I was battling spiritual doubt. By the looks on their faces, cancer might have been a less serious event. A lot of Christians can't handle the fact that some Christians (perhaps many) do indeed go through times of doubt.

To most churches I knew, doubting meant you simply didn't have enough faith. It meant you were bitter and needed to repent. I know some people who actually got laughed at when they told someone in their church they were walking through a season of doubt. Many Christians hate to see other Christians doubting. But for me, doubting didn't end in spiritual tragedy.

Looking back, I firmly believe that I had to doubt before I could believe again. I needed to ask questions—the hard questions, the questions that made no sense, the questions for which everybody else seemed to have perfect answers. I needed to discover those answers for myself. I wanted to let my spiritual plate get cleaned. But it was really hard to get clean when no one really wanted to hear I was entertaining a new companion—*doubt*.

Experience

I found a small ray of hope in a friendship with a guy named Scott. He was a pastor, but he was a different kind of pastor than I was used to. He didn't mind people asking questions. He enjoyed the conversation whether or not you agreed with him. After attending his small church for a couple of weeks, I cautiously asked if I could meet with him.

Over coffee one afternoon, I told Scott my story. I told him I had been spoon-fed Christianity since I was four. Surprisingly to me, he could relate. I told him I had never questioned "truth" before this year. I also told him that suddenly—through many questions about my childhood theology, doctrine, and life in general—Jesus didn't make sense to me anymore. As I spoke those words out loud to him, I found it very difficult to admit my doubt in something or someone who I believed in wholeheartedly for so long.

When I finished my long story, Scott looked up from his coffee cup and smiled. "Matthew, the story you are describing is not unlike many stories of people who grow up in the church," said Scott. "I'm sure your head is full of knowledge of the Bible, I'm sure you know what 'salvation' means, but it sounds like to me you can't look back and see a specific time where you *experienced* truth before."

"How can I experience truth?" I asked, thinking it sounded like another formula. If he was going to give me the spiritual equivalent to the quadratic equation, I didn't want to hear it. I was expecting him to give me some Jesus pamphlet, or worse yet, something outlining thirty days to experiencing truth. I didn't want that.

But for once in my life, a church person actually pleasantly surprised me.

"You can't force an experience with truth," said Scott. "You can certainly ask Jesus to make himself known to you, but truth is not something you can force anyone to see or feel. Only Jesus can make truth real to someone. To experience truth isn't to understand everything, so don't expect that to happen."

"Have you ever felt what I'm feeling?" I asked. "I know you've been to seminary and all that, but have you ever doubted in Jesus?"

"Of course." Scott's glance became fiery and passionate. It was like he was using his demeanor and not simply his words to get me to understand what he was getting ready to say. "Doubt is a part of believing. I'm not really sure you can truly believe in Jesus unless you wrestle with him a bit. And I think Jesus welcomes that. In fact, I think he sometimes likes it."

"But where does doctrine and theology come into all of this?" I asked.

"Matthew, you shouldn't mix doubt with doctrine," laughed Scott. "That's like fire coming into contact with gasoline. I think if you were to ask Jesus to clear your heart and mind of all the Christian jargon and all the Christian 'stuff' you have been accustomed to in the past, he *will* reintroduce himself to you."

"Scott, I have to tell you; I hate where I am right now," I said honestly. "I don't want to doubt, and honestly I'm afraid to be here in this place. I feel like God is going to zap me or something. I feel like I'm failing the Gospel by doing this."

Scott laughed.

"He's not going to *zap* you for doubting. Matthew, that's poorly taught Christianity influencing you; that's not Jesus. Stop panicking. Use this experience of doubt to fuel your desire to experience truth. Jesus will show up; I believe that with all of my heart. But remember, doubt will always be with us until we can see with our own eyes the glory of Jesus. But use it to ignite a desire within you to know truth."

Scott's words contented my soul, as cheesy as this might seem. I could breathe freely again. I wish I could say the following months were simple—they weren't. They were complicated and hard, but they were also life changing.

You're blessed when you've worked up a good appetite for God.
He's food and drink in the best meal you'll ever eat.

Matthew 5:6 The Message

The Genesis to a Journey

After my meeting with Scott, I did something quite drastic: I stopped going to church. I still met with Scott on occasion. But the church experience had become nauseating to me, and I believed it to be detrimental at that time to my desire to experience truth. I didn't want to hear all the beautiful "inspired" testimonies. I didn't want to be around all of the other people who had no questions. I didn't even want to shake hands with the welcoming guy who made life seem like it was a perfect little fairy tale. My decision to not go raised a few eyebrows; my parents were certainly concerned, but I knew it was the right thing for me to do—at least, for a time.

Instead of church, Jesus and I met one-on-one. I began to read, study, contemplate, and think about stories of Jesus. I *ignored* Paul. And I *ignored* Abraham. All I wanted to do was focus on Jesus, the things that he said and the things that he did. So, I poured my energy into relearning Jesus through the Gospels. I reread his stories, his relationships, his purpose. I wanted to reconnect with what he was passionate about. I wanted to rediscover why he died for me. For once in my life, I wanted to feel the truth and not just say it out loud. I wanted to pursue Jesus in hope that I would experience truth. But for much of that time, a part of me was scared I might not feel anything, and I didn't know what that was going to mean for my faith.

While Jesus and I met, I had many questions and concerns and doubts that would float through my mind. I would always take those thoughts and ideas and lay them out on a table in front of people I respected. Then we'd argue and fight, with my concept of Jesus hanging in the balance. Many times I walked away from those experiences knowing what I believed, but still not ready to claim the beliefs as my own.

Over time, I did begin to reconnect with my faith. But I was careful not to say that I believed something until I was able to own it. Despite all the knowledge I was gleaning from the Gospels, I hadn't felt like an experience had occurred.

Four months after my vacation from church began, I realized something about my experience with truth. Two weeks before that day, I had lost my grandmother. She would have been ninety-one on her next birthday. For the funeral, I had written down a few words; I stood beside her open casket and read my thoughts out loud to the roomful of people who were there to celebrate her life. What I had written was all about her faith, her joy, her love for life, and her love for Jesus. Only a few short days after her funeral, I went back to college.

As I sat on my dorm room bed two weeks after Mammom's funeral, the weight of her death only then began to seep in. I sat there contemplating all that she had meant to me. She had invested so much of herself into my life. I had no memory of her not being full of love and peace and joy. Everything she had was always there for my taking.

As all of those thoughts of my grandmother crashed through my brain, Jesus let me see a picture of truth. In that moment I realized I *had indeed experienced* truth as a child. I had just never recognized it. Because it wasn't in the church where I experienced it.

For as long as I could remember, I saw the truth of Jesus lived out in the life of my grandmother. To me, she was like the walking, breathing words of Jesus. My grandmother was an example of what the resurrection of Jesus did in a person. She was evidence that Jesus was truth. For me, truth had always been a list of things that I believed in. But I rarely thought about looking for the proof of truth in the lives of people.

Up until that day, just two weeks after I lost my grandmother, I had never understood what it meant to experience truth.

Sure, I had gotten a rather ugly view of Jesus from the church I grew up in. But Jesus had also given me hundreds of opportunities to *experience* his truth through the lives of people who were closest to me. People whose lives depicted his words and teachings and resurrection. *Truth* as an experience in my life turned out to be a very different picture than I would have ever anticipated.

But my time away from the church allowed me to see that picture. It wasn't simply the emotion of my grandmother's passing that led me to the place where I realized my experience with truth. It was in the beginning steps of relearning Jesus that I was able to open my heart and mind wide enough to let him come inside through ways that I wasn't accustomed to feeling.

I didn't walk away from that experience without questions. I didn't understand everything. I may have not had the best church upbringing, but because my grandmother, along with many other people in my life, chose to live out truth, I have never questioned the truth of Jesus again.

Realizing I had experienced the truth of Jesus through my grandmother helped put me on the journey with Jesus. It also made me want to embrace the teachings of Jesus in Matthew 5. But truth is only the beginning of freedom. On that day, two weeks after my grandmother's death, I realized my desperate need to relearn what it meant to follow Jesus.

That day was thirteen years ago.

I know now not to think of my faith in Jesus as a destination. The magic I experience in Jesus doesn't happen when I'm living a destination faith. Whenever I feel like I have arrived in my faith, Jesus quickly pushes me back onto the journey.

He continues to push me.

And he pushes hard.

6

light

As far as we can discern, the sole purpose of human existence is to kindle a light in the darkness of mere being.

Carl Jung, Swiss psychologist

Stopped in My Tracks by Light

"Daniel, I got stopped by a cop this morning," I said casually, as I dropped three packets of Equal into my unsweetened iced tea. I hate Equal, actually. But I like my iced tea sweet. That's one of only three reasons I like living in the South: sugar-drenched tea. *Mmm.*

"I was driving down on Highway 123 in McLean," I continued. "He pulled me over. Gosh, I was pissed."

My good friend Daniel was only half paying attention to my story; he was much more interested in the menu. He and I had just finished working at our church's youth group where he was the church's student ministry director; I was simply a volunteer. After our gig, we would usually grab a bite at Outback Steakhouse. Because he had spent nearly a year in Australia, Daniel had an undying affection for anything remotely "Down Under."

"Why did the cop stop you?" Daniel finally asked. "By the way, I think I'm getting the Chicken on the Barbie."

"OK, I think I'm getting the Outback special." Whenever my mind wasn't on food, I would almost always get the special—no thinking required. For someone who is constantly haunted by lurking ADHD, no thinking is always a good thing.

"So, why did the *cop* stop you?" asked Daniel again, getting somewhat impatient.

"He said I was going 45 in a 30. But I could have sworn that I had just looked at the speedometer and I was going 37. He said 45 and then gave me a $75 ticket."

"Wow. That stinks," said Daniel somewhat sarcastically. Which was pretty normal for Daniel; sarcasm dripped through him like water through ground coffee beans—slow and purposeful. "What time of day was it?"

"Dude, it was like seven in the morning. I didn't think I would have to worry about a cop on 123 that early in the day. Especially on a *Sunday!*"

"You always have to worry about a cop on 123," said Daniel. "It's like taxes and death. You know, certain."

Then, suddenly, Daniel looked at me with a quizzical look on his face—as if he was thinking to himself that something didn't add up.

"Matthew, what were you doing in McLean on 123 at seven in the morning on a Sunday?" he asked quickly, laughing a bit at the scenario.

light

I just looked at him.

Daniel had just asked me the one question I did not want to answer. I didn't feel like I could answer it—not without admitting I had slept over at my girlfriend's house the night before. I was certain that would be an extremely disappointing fact to Daniel, the friend who supposedly kept me accountable.

My girlfriend and I hadn't had sex, though we had certainly done more than simply kiss. As soon as Daniel found out where I had been, he was going to feel obligated to ask me a lot of questions—questions, frankly, I would not feel like answering.

My mind raced to find a quick remedy to my situation. *What am I going to say? What lie am I going to tell to my good friend Daniel?* As I sat scanning my brain for a good story, it felt as if God had emptied my mind of any reasonable lie that might have been convincing to my friend. Still trying my best to stay calm, I could think of no good reason for being in McLean on 123 at seven in the morning on a Sunday—*except for the truth.*

Meanwhile, Daniel was looking back at me with an incredulous grin on his face. "Did I ask a bad question?" he said, taking a sip of his drink.

"Umm . . . I, uh . . ." The syllables were stumbling out of me like I was scared out of my mind. The truth about myself didn't scare me. Telling another Christian the truth about me—that's what terrified me.

I didn't mind telling Jesus my problems; he was patient and friendly and known for his forgiveness. But every time I ever told another Christian, some kind of formula or process or preconceived judgment ensued before "forgiveness" would be made official. And most times, that forgiveness had a waiting period—I'd have to get approved, sign a contract, and then wait ten days for it to be made legit. I didn't like the process.

But at that moment, I was sick and tired of fearing the official business. Besides, the weight of what I carried *was* consuming my thoughts. So, I took a deep breath, and I just said it out loud with confidence.

"I was at my girlfriend's house. I stayed at her house last night."

Daniel just looked at me.

I felt the need to explain just a bit more.

"We didn't have sex," I said. "We've *never* done that. We don't want to do that . . . I mean *we do*, but we're not. That I can promise you. But we certainly weren't innocent . . .

"I was on my way from her house when I got the ticket. I was speeding because I was late for Sunday school."

Daniel was silent.

His forty-seven seconds of nonreply was too much for me to bear, so I broke the silence.

"Are you going to say something?" I asked seriously. "Do you hate me? I am *so* sorry, bro . . . I know I should have told you . . ."

Another minute went by, but to me it felt like twenty. Finally, Daniel piped up.

"Hate you? Do you *really* think I would hate you over something like this?" asked Daniel.

I shook my head no. But actually, I wasn't too sure of the answer to that question.

"You don't *ever* have to apologize to me. As long as I know that you and Jesus are talking through this stuff, I am fine. And by the look on your face, Jesus seems to be speaking rather clearly right now . . . Listen bro, I am your friend; I'm here to be a light when you can't 'find your way home,'" said Daniel, using both of his hands to motion air quotes. "Heck, I would expect the same from you."

light

As Daniel spoke, my eyes began to well up with tears. I'm not sure if it was his response or the heaviness that had just been lifted from my heart, but something moved me. I had rarely experienced "light" like this before. Everything in my spiritual history made me believe judgment was an extensive and critical part of light, especially the kind of light that shined inside the church walls. At first, Daniel's reaction to my sin confession felt very awkward and strange—like a foreign object I didn't understand. A part of me believed I needed to feel the judgment before I could experience the forgiveness of Christ.

After we ate, the two of us prayed. As I drove away, I said out loud in the car, "Jesus, help me remember this; I need to remember this experience. Light doesn't require judgment, and it should be done with mercy."

Daniel and I spent many times praying together over the next few months. His time and care and words were much-needed light for me, a desperate traveler.

When the light of Jesus shines through humanity, you never know what it will reveal.

You're here to be light, bringing out the God-colors in the world. God is not a secret to be kept. We're going public with this, as public as a city on a hill. If I make you light-bearers, you don't think I'm going to hide you under a bucket, do you? I'm putting you on a light stand.

Matthew 5:14–15 The Message

Christians Need Light

I've heard a lot of chatter about light over the years. Some of it has interested me. Some of it has not. Theologians and preachers, thinkers and poets, writers and musicians have long spent their

139

energy and talent playing in the sandbox with the concept of light. They ask questions: What is it? How do we show it? Is this way more effective than that? What did Jesus mean when he called us to be light in a dark world?

This kind of questioning isn't new; it's been happening since Jesus left earth. I think it's important and imperative to bring new understanding to the words of Jesus. But I must admit, it does frustrate me when people try to pass off their concept as something new. When I hear such statements, I often think of Solomon's words: "There's nothing new under the sun."

I don't have any new theories on light. I don't really have any regurgitated old theories either. All I have is what I have experienced. Just like you, I look to Scripture, prayer, and the words of all those thinkers who are much wiser than me to help me understand how I can be a more effective light for Jesus. When on a journey with Jesus, he teaches about light.

Like salt, light can be good and bad. You can reveal too much. You can shine too little. Sometimes we're called to be a spotlight. Other times, Jesus simply needs the gentle glow of candlelight. Those of us who have grown up in Christianity have been inundated with thousands of ideas and illustrations as they relate to being light.

The geography of where we're supposed to be light often gets debated. I hear the majority of modern Christians talk about the importance of *being* a light in the world. They believe Jesus's goal for us is to take the message to those who do not know him. "We are the light in the dark places; we need to be sharing the salvation message wherever we can," I heard one man say recently.

And I wholeheartedly agree with all of the people who make this their intent. Because I, too, think it's obvious Jesus was re-

light

ferring to evangelism in Matthew 5 when he said that he wanted us to be like a city on a hill. But I don't think evangelism is all he was talking about; I think our light is supposed to shine for anyone who is in need of knowing simple truth, feeling grace, or experiencing generous mercy. I think Jesus intended our light to shine for *all* to see.

I've heard many people unintentionally demean those who feel called to shine light in the church. "You're preaching to the choir," the critics will often say. I'm guilty of using that phrase too. Quite frankly, it's sometimes appropriate. Some people do spend too much of their time inside the safety of the church. But I don't think it helps the cause of Jesus to spend time criticizing such people.

A few years ago, I had a motto for being light: pursue shining it out into the world. I went out of my way to only pursue relationships with people who had no concept of Jesus. When I was around these individuals, I shined Jesus as best as I could. I was careful not to assume every person was the same. I invested a great deal of thought into knowing where they were and how I could be most effective at being a light in their lives. But I ended up getting drained—mentally, spiritually, and emotionally. Oftentimes when you're concentrating on *being* light, you forget that you have to take the time to look for light too. It dawned on me one day *I* needed light. I needed to see the city on a hill just as much as those who didn't know Jesus needed to see that same city. I needed the light of other believers to shine on me so I could continue to shine. All of us need to see and experience some good light.

When I experience light, I am experiencing the story of Christ lived out through the lives of others. I don't know about you, but it thrills me to see Jesus come alive through friends, family, and strangers.

beatitude

Last year, one of my closest and dearest friends, Lee Steffen, left Nashville to travel the world helping people. I was sad to see him leave the area; many times he had been the local friend who was my sounding board, prayer partner, and fellow dreamer.

But since he's set out on his journey, I have looked for and anticipated his light. Through phone calls, e-mails, and his personal blog, I have gotten to see the God-colors of this world in a way I would have never witnessed had he not taken this huge leap of faith and followed his heart. Lee's light, all the things his life communicates about Jesus, fills me up so I can continue to dream, live, and shine Jesus in this world.

Jesus called me to be light. He said for me to not hide it. He said for me to be like a city on a hill. I don't want to be afraid to be that city for both those who believe and those who resist the truth. My friend Daniel reminded me of this by letting Jesus shine through his words that night at Outback. Despite stumbling upon a dark place in my life, he didn't avoid letting me have a glimpse of the light he knew to be true. And I desperately needed to see it.

The church is too often filled with dark places in need of light to appear. Magic happens when we proactively look for opportunities to reveal Jesus in the situations where we live. All we need to do is look to see where God can use us to reach people in need of light. If we let ourselves be used, light works.

Flexible

Ocean City, Maryland, is usually a place one goes when they are in search of the warm summer sunshine and mostly naked bodies. But on this particular trip, I wasn't there for the sunshine and ocean water; it was November, and one of the largest seventh- and eighth-grade youth retreats in the country was in town. I had made the trip over from Northern Virginia to be a youth leader. Up until that day, I had never really interacted much with seventh- and eighth-graders. However, all of that was about to change as I had been chosen to be the "adult" in one of the hotel rooms where I would be sharing a space with five seventh-grade boys. I had no idea what I was about to encounter.

The experience was less than thrilling for me.

"Did you know that you are going bald?" asked one of the kids bluntly.

"I am? *I had no idea,*" I said, somewhat sarcastically. However, my words were much nicer than my thoughts. I had just recently come to terms with the fact that my hairline was making a beeline for my backside. Denial was still a little bit of a problem for me at that time. I hated that I was going bald, and I was already thinking way too much about it on the inside. Needless to say, I wasn't ready to discuss my hair's desolate future in an open forum—especially with a bunch of harsh seventh-graders.

"Do you use Rogaine?" the kid continued.

"That's none of your business," I said.

The kid started laughing out loud.

"That means you do," he joked.

He then pointed to his friend who was jumping ferociously on one of the beds and said, "Hey, Dan, this guy uses Rogaine."

"He needs to, Kevin," said Dan. "If he doesn't, he'll have trouble with the ladies. All bald men have trouble with the ladies."

I thought about retaliating, but I didn't think it would have a point. Again, they were seventh-graders. So, instead, I self-consciously and covertly checked my hairline out in the mirror, hoping I would feel better. It didn't help.

Then, out of the blue, the conversation among the kids changed.

"How many people think our math teacher, Mr. Dyson, is gay?"

asked Dan, yelling so he could be heard over the commotion of the room.

"Dan, we don't need to be discussing that here," I said in a fatherly tone. I hate hearing myself speak in that tone.

"He's *totally* gay," said Kevin.

The others piped up and agreed.

"Well, that's for him to worry about and not us," I said, trying desperately to think up a new subject.

"*Hey, guys!*" yelled Kevin. "*Let's look and see if our TV gets porn.* Maybe we have *Skinamax!*"

"*Sit down, Kevin*; you're not looking to see if the TV gets porn," I snapped. Kevin didn't turn on the TV, but he continued to test my patience.

"Hey, Matthew, have you ever had oral sex?" Kevin asked, running back over to jump on the bed.

"*What?!*" I replied.

"You know, *oral sex!*" Kevin said indifferently. The thirteen-year-old kid then went on to name off about six other names for it—two of which I had never heard before. He acted as if I had never heard of it before.

"Kevin, I know what it is; I just don't think this is the place to be talking about that. OK?" I was firm, but tried not to be a complete geek. Although I felt like I was thoroughly failing.

"Well, I can't wait to get my first . . ." said Kevin and then he proceeded to simulate the motion of receiving oral sex.

"*Kevin, what are you doing?*" I screamed, pushing him off the bed. "*We are at a Christian retreat; we don't act like that.*"

I am not made for this, God.

Though I may have come a long way from the stifled bubble of my conservative Christian school education, I still had little clue about the culture of public school kids. These five kids said *many* things that my publisher will not let me write on these pages. At the time, I was not used to this behavior. The youth groups I had helped with before were filled with kids who had been churched and overchurched since they were in diapers. With those kids, ministry seemed easy; they still had the church's idea of innocence and truth very much intact. I had *never* been shocked by what came out of their mouths. But the five boys I stayed with at that retreat were much more informed about the world than I would have ever imagined. Sadly, in certain instances, they were much more informed than me.

After we returned from the weekend retreat, the youth pastor asked me if I would lead a seventh- and eighth-grade small group. I was more than a little hesitant at first. I didn't think I was made for the "seventh-and-eighth-grade" kind of light. But the youth pastor persisted and encouraged me to take a leap of faith and participate.

Finally, I agreed. But I wasn't excited about it.

For three years, every Sunday morning at 11 a.m., I gathered with a group of eight rambunctious teenagers and talked to them about God, life, girls, and sex. At first I was forceful and rigid, which caused two kids to leave the group. That's when the youth pastor told me I needed to be flexible and not try and force stuff down the throats of these kids. He told me if I would simply back away and let God's light shine through me, good results would come.

So, I pursued being an adaptable sort of light—whatever that really means.

During those three years, sometimes all we did was go to Starbucks and chat. *That was hard at first.* Other times we opened our Bibles and searched God's Word for clues about what life is truly about. Eventually, I got used to them making fun of me going bald.

When they jokingly brought up oral sex or masturbation, I let them talk about it, and then I tried to figure out a way to bring God into the conversation. Sometimes it was successful; sometimes it was disastrous. Sometimes it was light-filled.

When I left the Northern Virginia area, those guys were in the ninth and tenth grades. The night before I left, they took a picture of all of us. One of the kids' mothers had it framed and sent it to me in Nashville. I still have that picture. Over the years, I have often looked at the picture and whispered a prayer for each of those boys. I hoped someone was being light in their lives.

Last year I had the pleasure of being the speaker for that church's youth retreat. Most of the guys who had been in my small group were in college by then. When I walked into the youth pastor's office, a mother who was going to be volunteering on the trip followed me in.

"Hi, I'm Mary," she said.

"Mary, this is Matthew Turner," said the youth pastor. "He's speaking this weekend."

"You're *the* Matthew Turner?" said Mary loudly. "I have *heard all about* you."

"Really? You have?"

"Oh, gosh, yeah. I am pretty much Kevin's second mom," she said. "He was in your small group. Do you remember Kevin?"

"Of course, I remember."

"You influenced him more than you will ever know. I want you to know that. In fact, he'll be at the retreat this weekend. He's coming up from his West Virginia university to volunteer."

Her words made my heart sing a bit. I didn't say anything out loud, but inside I was dancing a little. It felt good—maybe even *magical.*

When I arrived at the retreat, it was awesome to see Kevin again.

light

He's pursuing his love of Jesus with fervor and hasn't lost any of the vibe that made him so unique. Another guy from my small group, John, contacted me via instant messenger recently just to say hello. He, too, is chasing his dreams in light of the story God has written on his heart. Dan, on the other hand, hasn't been back to church since he was in tenth grade. The last time I heard from him, he was investing life into other "things" more important to him. But Kevin, John, and Dan are not the reason why I share this story. You learn on the journey that light isn't something that can be measured in successes and failures.

This story is about how sometimes our light has to take on different forms to be effective. Being light is less about the message and more about the person who is watching you. For some people, light comes in the form of honesty. For others, they see it in simple acts of kindness. And for others, they just need a hug.

For the young men in my small group, they wanted to know if a twenty-something guy who's losing his hair could relate to their story. And before I could relate to the stories of these young men, I had to step away from my preconceived ideas about good behavior. I had to alter my preplanned schemes about what spiritual investment looked like. I had to understand that being light doesn't play by my rules of comfort.

Ultimately, I chose to venture out and let Jesus use me in a situation that didn't come naturally to me. My decision didn't instantly make me relate or feel comfortable. Change took time. I learned to adjust the light according to the situation at hand. Did I see a lot of magic happen during those few years? Not really. And for a long time, I thought I was wasting my time. But today, when I'm busy writing on my computer and one of my old small group guys sends me an instant message to say hello, to let me know what God is doing in his life . . . that's when I experience the magic. You give light, you get light back.

However, they do still make fun of me for losing my hair.

Nobody Said It Would Be Easy

As soon as I picked up my cell phone, I knew by the sound of Daniel's voice he wasn't calling me with good news. I had been waiting for him at a restaurant. He was running late—with good reason.

"Matthew, I can't come to dinner; Jennifer committed suicide this afternoon," said Daniel, obviously fighting back tears. "She hung herself."

"*What?!* Are you kidding me?"

Of course, I knew he wasn't kidding. Decent people don't kid about stuff like that. Unfortunately, I didn't know Jennifer all that well; all I knew was that she was a fourteen-year-old girl who occasionally attended my church's youth group. As I listened to Daniel describe the few details that he knew, my mind raced back to three weeks before when I had lost a cousin and two friends in an unforgettable series of events on a Memorial Day weekend. Every death had been separate, tragic, and unexpected. My cousin had died of an aneurism, my friend in a car accident, and a kid I knew from work had taken his own life. The experience of losing that many people all at once made my own life seem somewhat overrated.

To say the least, that Memorial Day weekend had left me with a lot of questions.

As the news of Jennifer's death traveled, my cell phone began to ring incessantly. But I chose not to pick up the calls. I didn't feel like chatting anymore. So, instead, I began to nervously pace the restaurant parking lot, talking audibly at God.

light

"Is this your idea of taking care of things?" I asked, as kindly and respectfully as I could. Questioning God was a new concept for me, but I had recently stumbled upon new grace that allowed me to ask questions—freely. "You just decided to take someone else? Please tell me where I am supposed to see faithfulness and mercy in this. Please? I don't see you answering anybody's prayer."

I knew God had the power to intervene and save someone's life if he wanted to. And the fact that he didn't frustrated me. When my cousin collapsed in front of a toilet and was rushed to the hospital, we had thousands of people praying God would bring him through his sickness. But the miraculous never happened. Then, when I had heard the kid I worked with went missing at a Christian retreat he was on, thousands of people had prayed for his safe return. The next day his body was discovered on the ground near a broken limb and some rope. God had seemingly been absent from the situation. Or at least, that's what I thought at the time.

While pacing and talking, my cell phone rang again; this time it was Lisa, a fellow volunteer in the youth ministry. Lisa and I had been friends for a few years now.

"Lisa, I am so sorry," I said as soon as I answered the call. To me, a regular "hello" just didn't seem appropriate.

Lisa said nothing at first; the only thing I could hear was the sound of her sniffling nose in my ear.

"I wish I had the words to say to help make you feel better, but I don't," I said quietly.

There were no good words to say, really. Nobody has anything good to say in this kind of a situation. That balance between saying something and saying nothing at all is a very tangled web. In a moment like that, everything you say seems shallow and stupid, but when you say nothing, it seems careless and unresponsive. Sometimes to a fault, I almost always choose speaking.

"I have a question," said Lisa. "Where do you think God is?"

"I don't know!" I replied in frustration. "Where *is* God in this situation? I've just spent the last fifteen minutes asking him that same question. Where was he three weeks ago when my cousin died? Where was he today when Jennifer tied a noose in her room?"

Lisa interrupted me.

"Mateo," said Lisa; she always found the need to call me by the Spanish equivalent of my name. I'm still not sure why. "I think we're asking different questions."

Lisa was getting ready to jet off on one of her intellectual spiritual tangents; I was sure of it. Her intelligence was far above the average church attendee. It's not as though she flaunted it like others I knew; she simply *was* intelligent, and therefore her faith benefited. I have to admit, Lisa usually made a good point.

"*Your* questions imply God is not here," said Lisa. "*I* was just asking where you thought he might show up. Where he exists. I am sure he exists in this tragedy. Wherever he is, I want to make him more known, that's all."

"Oh. I don't have the faintest idea, Lisa," I said. "Honestly, I don't really understand any of this. It seems completely absent-minded of God to allow this to happen again in my life."

"Again, I think you might be missing the point, Matthew," said Lisa carefully. "This situation *isn't* really about you. The deaths that happened several weeks ago, although tragic and close to you, weren't about you, either. I just happen to believe that God shows up, and it's our job to reveal him to the best of our ability. That's what being light is about . . ."

Lisa's words silenced me. With the phone against my ear, leaning up against a stranger's van, I simply listened.

light

". . . Do you know how many people are going to need to see Jesus in the events of the next three days? Hundreds. Are we going to stand here and ask a bunch of questions we may never know the answer to, or are we going to go do what we're called to do? I think we need to be light, Matthew. We need to encourage, pray, and support. A lot of kids are going to need our help to get through this."

Sadly, I have a selfish habit of always trying to find the shortest distance between tragedy and how it relates to me. Actually, I do that with most things.

Lisa was right. This tragedy wasn't about me. God didn't owe me any explanation. He didn't have to answer all of my questions about why he didn't intervene. If I truly loved him, if I truly desired to be used, then I would simply concentrate my life and actions and energy on what he expected of me. That didn't mean it would be easy; it was simply the story he chose to write in my life. I needed to comply. One of the greatest reminders from Jesus on the journey was this: this life isn't about me. It isn't about my story. That was extremely hard for me to learn.

Lisa reminded me light was the one thing we could offer without having all of the pieces to the puzzles. We didn't have to understand the whys and hows of this event to be light. She said we needed to focus on being simple candles of peace, prayer, and hope to all the people who would be asking questions and facing sadness during this time. So, that's what we tried to do; Lisa and I focused on being light.

But knowing where to shine light proved a little difficult. Eventually, our light was most effective in Daniel's life. The next few days proved overwhelming for our friend. He felt the weight of being a comforter and companion and pastor to hundreds of people dealing with a needless tragedy. But through this situation, Lisa and I kept focusing on Daniel to keep his heart and mind on truth. We prayed for Daniel. We laid hands on Daniel. Sure, I didn't understand why the power of Jesus hadn't been revealed for Jennifer. But I chose to believe in Jesus's power for Daniel despite my feelings and questions. We prayed that power over Daniel's life. In the end, Jesus used him miraculously over the course of those few days. Surely, Jesus was in the situation, and Daniel simply helped make him known. Lisa and I helped make him known to Daniel. He needed to see the city on the hill. We tried our best, through grace, to be like a city.

Those tragedies happened several years ago. Today, I still find the idea of being light to be complicated and difficult. At times, it's downright impossible for me to even think about revealing Jesus in a situation. But I want to. I want to learn how to make that something I pursue every day. Why? Because I believe in it. I believe in what light does in the lives of other people. It's my desire to be one flickering light in a huge city. When my light is dim, it's my prayer that Jesus makes yours all the brighter. Because I hope when I see your light I will be encouraged to shine again when my life gets hard. Likewise, when you see my little candle shining brightly among thousands of others, I hope it encourages you to continue shining, to continue being a part of the city, the city that is giving faraway travelers the welcoming sight of home.

Lisa shined light on me. Together, we shined light on Daniel, and he was given the chance to shine light on thousands—some who believed and some who did not.

It's still often befuddling to me how the soft glow of a candle can be magical. But when I think about what it looks like for a traveler, when they see thousands and thousands of candles

light

softly glowing against a hillside—that sight brings hope to them for rest, food, and water. For some, it might even bring about thoughts of home and safety. When I think *those* thoughts, I am reminded about how magical the light of Jesus shining through people can be.

7

humility

Humility is like underwear, essential, but indecent if it shows.

Helen Nielsen, author

Four Eyes and a Topography Map

I've been humbled more than a few times in my life.

My father has always liked things three ways: fast, close, and cheap. He's never been much for waiting in a line unless he's at the Bass Pro Shop. He can't stand driving more than seven miles to any place unless he's going hunting. And he refuses to ever pay full price unless he's buying a new shotgun. As a kid, I was mostly OK with my dad's stiff way of doing things. But once in a while, his self-made creed would seep far enough into my little world that it would interfere with my noblest attempts to be cool.

Just like my father had a creed, when I was a teenager I had a three-point belief statement about life too. I believed I wanted to be cool. I believed I wanted others to think I was cool. I believed if I wasn't deemed cool by others, my life would be ruined.

The odds were stacked against me too. I was quite possibly the *uncoolest* individual at my high school, other than the boy with the constant body odor problem and the girl who would fall asleep in class and then talk out loud about the guys she was crushing on. "Cool" was very hard for me to come by.

My voice was high, my frame was frail, and I was about as coordinated as . . . well, take my word for it, I was *really* unco-ordinated. Needless to say, the girls didn't like guys with higher voices and smaller waists than them. And my dark brown, thick-rimmed eyeglasses didn't help my case for coolness and sex appeal, either.

I hardly remember being able to see without glasses. All three of my sisters had 20/20 eyesight. But not me! By the time I turned seven, I had already gone through two pair of eyeglasses. My personal motto was: if it's in my family *and* it's hereditary, I would end up with it.

As a kid, I was like the drain catcher at the bottom of the kitchen sink—although I outwardly had a good attitude about almost every-thing, I was thoroughly convinced God had a cruel way of showing how much he loved me.

When I was fourteen, I was long past due on getting a new pair of glasses when I entered the ninth grade. I was still wearing the gold metal-framed ones I had gotten when I was ten. One of my teachers had noticed me squinting and told me to tell my parents to get my eyes checked. Against my better judgment, Dad offered to take me to the doctor.

"Dad, has Mom set up an appointment with my eye doctor?" I asked.

"No, son; *I did*. I called and made you an appointment at the eye doctor in Still Pond. He's right down the street from us."

"Why can't I go to my regular doctor?"

"Eye doctors are all the same; it don't make any difference what one you go to."

"OK, if you say so. When am I going?"

"A week from this coming Wednesday."

"We couldn't get anything sooner?"

"The eye doctor only visits Still Pond on Wednesdays."

"What kind of doctor visits only on Wednesdays? Is he the one from *Little House on the Prairie*?" I asked sarcastically.

"It'll be fine, Matt. Joe from my office goes in there to see him."

"Joe doesn't even wear glasses, Dad."

"Then the doctor must be pretty good, huh?" My dad laughed. But I wasn't amused.

My entire high school career hung in the balance. I already had a voice that sounded like I was constantly inhaling helium; I couldn't afford to have ugly glasses too.

When a week from Wednesday had finally come, I visited the eye doctor—the one who was close and cheap. He didn't have to be fast; when something was cheap and close, it almost always made the "fast" part of Dad's creed obsolete.

When the doctor finished the checkup, he told us to go over and look at the selection of frames. We did. And there, right in front of Dad and me was a grand selection of twenty-seven styles of men's frames.

"Dad, all of these are really ugly."

"Just pick a pair."

"Dad, these are hideous. *Really* hideous!"

"*Pick* a pair, and let's get out of here. How about these? Put these on."

"They're so big; they cover my eyebrows."

"These?"

"*No!*"

I closed my eyes tightly and prayed. *Lord Jesus, please, when I open my eyes, help me to see a pair of frames that are at least somewhat cool.* I tried on all but one of the twenty-seven pair; I refused to even look at the ones that looked more like goggles than glasses. Per my father's creed, I ended up choosing the cheapest frames this little Still Pond office had to offer. They cost $39. And they were ugly, brown, large, and *ugly.*

After I had the glasses for a week or two, my dad sat me down and talked to me about *my* way.

"Life doesn't always go your way, son; in fact, it usually doesn't," said my dad with more conviction than I had ever felt in my short fourteen-year life. When Dad spoke, he had an unfettered passion I admired. I always looked at him when he talked; his presence demanded it. "You'll understand this one day. Not getting your way isn't easy, but it happens to all of us."

By the time I reached college, I should have been a professional at the concept of being humble. I was easily the most picked-on kid in high school. (Of course, that was other than the boy who had constant body odor and the girl who talked in her sleep.) My high school experiences had made me highly self-conscious. So, when I got to college, I felt like I had the chance to begin anew. At least, that's what I had wanted.

But college brought new trials. Not only did I battle a great amount of spiritual doubt during that time in my life, but I had another battle to contend with. In certain ways, this battle was harder than facing doubt. It was the battle I had proudly managed to elude all of my teenage years, the battle that, even thinking about it, made me shudder with fear, the battle that *really* made me fight my pride—*acne*.

By the time I reached my nineteenth year on earth, my face looked like a war zone. Across my forehead and over both sides of my face, I had what looked to be a topographical map of the Appalachian Trail.

Very few people understood my pain. It's not like some of them hadn't experienced acne—but they had been *fifteen* when it happened, not getting ready to hit the drinking age.

When I battled acne, everyone gave me the absolute worst advice on how to get rid of it. I never asked for the advice. But that didn't stop clear-skinned individuals from offering their best words on my complexion dilemma.

"I've heard that taking a blow-dryer and drying your acne every morning after you take a shower helps," said one girl.

"Don't *ever* pop your zits!" said *everybody*.

"Have you ever tried rubbing your face with a pee-filled baby diaper? I hear it really works."

"Before you go to bed, try putting toothpaste on your face."

"Have you ever tried egg whites?"

I tried every one of those home remedies, except one. There was no way I was going to rub a wet baby diaper on my face.

After countless remedies that didn't work, after yelling in front of the mirror more times than I can remember, after all of the clean-faced people's comments about my skin, I finally took drastic measures to handle my acne—makeup. Yes, makeup—*women's makeup*. I figured actors and singers wore makeup onstage to cover up blemishes. Why couldn't I?

So, I went to the drugstore and bought an oil-free bottle of foundation that was as close to my skin color as possible. I had decided if anyone ever asked me if I was wearing makeup, I would say, "It's a new acne medication that covers up and cleans up my face."

The makeup worked like a charm too. Well, it did until one of my college friends asked me in front of six other guys if I was wearing makeup.

Silence.

An insane feeling washed over me like I was suffering through one of the ten plagues of Egypt. *Wow!* I thought, *I remember this feeling; I had this feeling in high school. This is what humiliation feels like. It's been a while since I felt that kind of sting.*

"It's medication for my acne," I said with as much confidence as I could muster. Then I quietly and awkwardly walked out of my buddy's room, headed back to my own room and washed my face.

I walked into my dorm room a different man than I had walked out. Humiliation in front of one's peers changes a man. When your innermost circle knows your deepest secret, life is never quite the same. Nor should it be.

The makeup incident was never talked about again.

Humble Beginnings

I've had many moments in my life when I wanted to crawl underneath my bed and never come out. Once I sang "O Holy Night" on Christmas morning. The entire song was absolutely perfect until I reached the ending high note—the *really* high note—and my voice cracked (well, it actually shattered) in front of the entire church. Everybody laughed. Another time, I was hosting an event in front of a thousand people. When my name was introduced, I proudly walked across the stage, looking out at the large crowd, and then I tripped over a guitar cord and fell on my face. Everybody laughed.

humility

Humbling moments seem to follow me like my shadow. I guess in reality, they follow most people.

My family, friends, and I laugh at most of these moments now. They've become stories that are brought up around the Thanksgiving table or get remembered when old friends and I are catching up. They've been retold so many times I wonder if all of the details are even true. But my memory etches them into my history. They become a part of my identity. They become unforgettable.

I wish being humbled and embracing humility were the same. But they're not. In fact, they're quite different, almost opposites of each other. Enduring situations that put you in a humbling position is often a bad feeling; it's embarrassing and uncomfortable. But all of those situations that have left me feeling embarrassed pale in comparison to the times God has taught me what it means to live a life of humility.

Few things are more beautiful to me than a person who lives out humility. Meeting a lowly soul who strives with all of her heart at being last in the world is one of the most magical experiences I have lived. But a part of me hates these experiences. Through them God shows me a picture of myself that reveals my pride. Very little, in my opinion, brings us as much joy and sense of stability as pride. But nothing feels more humiliating and dirty than realizing I'm prideful. I hate feeling dirty almost as much as I hate being last.

Pride fuels much of my inability to embrace the teachings of Jesus, to embrace the lifestyle that emits the magic he desires to come out of my life. Most of the hardest lessons in my life come when I fight the inner need to please only me. But each experience with humility, each time I get a glimpse of the picture Jesus sees in me, I am faced with the decision of whether to surrender

161

to Jesus or continue depending on my ability. Pride tells me I can remain. Jesus says *move*. That, in essence, is the conflict of life. Jesus is constantly telling me to get out of his way. My will tells me to stand my ground. While many talk of Jesus's sweet whispers, I've grown accustomed to his loud, forceful tone urging me to stand down.

A Bad Taste of Humility in My Mouth

A few years ago, Daniel had to confront me. The two of us were doing our normal meal and drinks at Bob Evans, but this one had been planned with a purpose. Daniel was on an uncomfortable mission to talk with me *about me*. So while I was eating cinnamon pancakes in the afternoon, Daniel cleared his throat.

"I actually need to chat with you about something," he said seriously.

As soon as I heard those words, my heart rate increased 20 percent, my appetite left me, and Jesus told me to shut up and listen. I love when the attention is put on me, but not when it's bad attention. Bad attention stresses me out. Instantly, I became stressed. My hatred of surprises, especially ones involving my potential wrongdoing, kept me from keeping my mouth closed.

"*What did I do?*" I asked, rolling my eyes at the mere thought that we were having a conversation such as this one.

"Why are you taking a tone with me?" Daniel asked. "I haven't even said anything yet, and you're all ready to retaliate. This is pretty typical of you."

"OK. What did I do, Daniel?" I repeated myself, this time using a forced smile—and sweet tone to disguise my raging blood pressure. "I would certainly like to know what it is I did."

"Don't you think I will tell you?"

humility

"OK, I'm calm," I said, lying through my teeth.

"Two of my friends have made comments about you, Matthew," said Daniel gingerly. I listened intently as my then somewhat new friend carefully selected each word as it was coming out of his mouth. "They are offended by your conversations about sex. They find much of your talk to be inappropriate and unnecessary; they're tired of hearing the innuendos . . ."

As Daniel talked, a fight broke out inside my mind between me "the bastard" and me "the guy who was pursuing Jesus."

This has got to be a joke!
(Just listen to Daniel.)
How on earth could my conversation have offended
    someone?
(You talk about sex a lot.)
Sure, I'm an open person.
(Rude and inappropriate is more like it.)
What's wrong with talking about sex once in a while?
(Absolutely nothing with the right group of people. But you talk
    about it every chance you get. People get tired of that.)
Who among Daniel's friends are legalists?
(Does that really matter? Aren't you simply avoiding the problem
    with a question like that?)

Daniel continued as the war raged inside.

"They even went as far as to say that unless you changed, they don't want to hang out with you anymore."

Fine. I don't need friends like that anyway.
(Actually, you do. You only have, like, two friends. These are
    Daniel's friends, and you owe them an apology.)
I still can't believe that someone complained about me!

(Stop focusing on you. The whole world doesn't revolve around you. At least you have a friend who is willing to chat with you about it.)

Daniel kept talking. I just stared at him.

"And man, honestly, you need to think about how your conversation is viewed by God," said Daniel. "He's pretty clear about our words showcasing the condition of our hearts. Sometimes, the way you talk *is inappropriate.* It might be normal conversation where you came from, but it's not around my friends and me. And I don't think I'm being overly sensitive. Just talk to God about it, man."

Sure, Dan, bring God into this conversation. That's just great. Perfect!
(Daniel, way to bring God into this conversation . . . that's perfect. Nice transition!)

Daniel stopped talking. I waited a couple of minutes to respond.

"Wow!" I said, not knowing really how to reply. But not knowing how to respond certainly didn't stop me from trying. "Honestly, Daniel, a part of me wants to lash out and say your friends are full of crap. I think it's insane that I would make them feel uncomfortable. I realize I'm an open person, but I think it's a bit ridiculous."

Daniel shrugged his shoulders. "Then lash out, Matthew. What's stopping you?"

"But then I think, perhaps they're right. Perhaps I do take my conversations too far. Perhaps, in the course of running away so far from my legalistic past, I'm in a place where I'm taking the grace of Jesus for granted." I sat there for a second, quiet. "But I need to think about all of this."

humility

"And really, that's all I'm asking," Daniel said.

Our conversation humbled me, embarrassed me, and put me in my place, but eventually it led me to a place of humility, confession, and happier friends. Long before I could change my behavior, I had to see a picture of myself. I had to take myself off the pedestal. I had to realize this life story is not about me. God doesn't want me focusing on my story; he wants me to join his. If I decide to join his story, that means I have to be concerned for the thoughts of others.

Sadly, humility is not a onetime lesson. It's a place that you have to keep going back to again and again. The lessons get easier if you make the trip there yourself. But if you forget to go or you emphatically stop going, life will remind you. It might take years, but humility always comes around again.

Humility won't leave me alone. Thankfully, not every lesson is confrontational; sometimes it's simply in meeting a humble person Jesus knocks me off my throne and onto the floor.

Sometimes, humiliation is a beautiful thing.

God blesses those who are gentle and lowly, for the whole earth will belong to them.

Matthew 5:5

Wow

Something about Darlene Zschech moved me.

I've had the sincere pleasure of meeting many artists who make Christian music. I don't *just* get to meet them, usually; I often have a chance to engage them in conversation. In the past, I've taken this for granted; I try not to anymore. I realize now that, like a painter, a musician's job is to look at life and find a way to communicate its true meaning through art. Now, some

Christian artists do this well, while others are, to put it nicely, simply good singers.

But once in a while when I meet someone who creates music for a living, the conversation leaves a mark on me. I love when this happens. Because I realize that's the point of a true artist: when they do what artists are supposed to do, they inspire the rest of us.

Honestly, I didn't expect to be inspired by Darlene. When a colleague of mine and I sat down for a conversation with the writer of "Shout to the Lord," we were both a little skeptical, my colleague even more than I.

From the moment we sat down around a small table and began talking, Darlene's kindness and overall sense of spiritual maturity permeated the room. Several times during the conversation, I caught myself thinking, *What does this woman have that I don't, and where can I go and get it?*

Of course, a part of me was also thinking, *If I can actually sense the good in her life, can she sense the bad in mine? Does she know that she's sitting down with two cynical Christian music editors? Does she sense the sin in my life? Is this dear woman sickened by me?*

I didn't know it at the time, but my colleague felt it too. *And that was a big deal.* She was much more cynical than me. When she and I walked into the elevator after our interview was complete, she looked at me and asked, "Did you feel that?" I looked at her and shook my head yes. Simply put, something was extraordinarily different about Darlene, something magical that inspired me to walk away from our conversation feeling alive, on fire even.

My conversation with my colleague continued as we got in the car to leave. Both of us were still a bit dumbfounded.

humility

"What was it about her that is different from so many other artists we meet?" I asked. "It was insane."

"Matthew, *humility*," she said. "She was genuinely humble. I felt *dirty* next to her."

"*Me too*. I wanted to get 'saved' again."

"*I know*, but in all seriousness, I think she just knew Jesus—like *knows* on a different level than me. You could tell she had spent time with him—*more time than I have*."

I think my friend nailed it. Somewhere along Darlene's journey of faith, Jesus had taught her something about humbling herself in God's sight. I believe she went to that place often—as often as she could.

Something dawned on me that day regarding humility. I realized that humility accentuates our faith in Jesus. Darlene didn't have to tell me she knew Jesus; she didn't need to overexplain her stories or conjure up some message in hope of inspiring us. Because of her humility, her *life* inspired us. The message of Jesus was written all over her face.

So often, people who claim to be Christian, myself included, do so much to try and prove they indeed have the light of Jesus shining in them.

We Christians like to advertise that we're Christian. There have been times in my life when I have *loved* letting people know I was Christian. But more often than not, when we go out of our way to impress someone with our spiritual knowledge or our good deeds or our bright lights, our faith is dimmed because of our pride.

That makes a lot of sense. When less of me actually exists in the picture, when I'm not so quick to promote my story, Jesus gets a chance to break through my life and he tells my story for me. Or better yet, he gets a chance to use me to tell his. The question usually comes down to this: am I humble enough to let him do either?

I guess it depends on whether or not I am looking for magic. Humility takes my will, my needs, my goals out of the story—that's hard. Sometimes Jesus comes and makes that change for you—that's very hard.

The Changing Face of Humility

Shortly after losing my job as the editor of *CCM**, I had a long conversation with Lisa, who tends to be blatantly honest, about humility. She and I met up at Starbucks in Northern Virginia. (I was back in the area on vacation.)

"He's got you pegged, Mateo," said Lisa, laughing. I had just told her a story about my recent visit with a friend who is also a therapist. He had jokingly diagnosed me as a "self-centered bastard."

"Seriously, Mateo," said Lisa, "that is hilarious! And actually, he might not be too far off."

"What are you saying?"

"I'm saying I think he has a point. You sometimes are *self-centered*. And sometimes, you're a bastard."

Lisa is one of only a handful of people who can get away with calling me self-centered. Everybody calls me a bastard at least once and means it.

"You're lucky you are leaving for Romania soon," I said. "That's all I got to say. If you weren't going to serve Jesus in a foreign land, we'd be officially not talking right now." I smiled.

"Man, it's good to see you again, Mateo," laughed Lisa.

"You too."

This was a normal conversation between Lisa and me. It was quite common for us to sit around for a couple of hours and talk about everything from the weather to movies to our significant oth-

---

* In *Provocative Faith*, I shared the story about losing my job as the editor of the Christian music magazine *CCM*. This event was a defining moment in my professional life, and my spiritual life too. It ended up helping me on the journey with Jesus.

ers. By the time we finished gabbing, our butts were numb from sitting too long. Most of our talks revolved around wrestling with the things of God. This was how we learned more. This was how we sharpened each other. We didn't think we had all of the answers. But that didn't stop us from leaning on each other's knowledge for support. For us, this was the meaning of community.

"What's God been teaching you lately?" asked Lisa, stirring her teacup and breathing in its steam.

"Well, it's kind of ironic that I got my official 'diagnosis,'" I said, laughing. "Because lately Jesus has been teaching me humility."

"Really? Since you lost your big *CCM* job?"

"Yeah, it's been really hard, Lisa. When you lose a job that you pretty much built your world around, it tends to hit you where it hurts. But I've learned a ton through this—humility is tied to so much of my life that this was probably exactly what I needed to learn. With me getting married next year, I'm sure it will be helpful to have really learned a good lesson in humility."

"I'm sure you will learn a lot of lessons in humility—for the rest of your life."

"Yeah, I hope so; I think I'm finally learning how much I need humility in my life. It's so easy for me to think all of this I do is about me."

"Are you doing better now?"

"I'm better. Once I realized my world wasn't over, and Jesus truly needed to teach me a lesson, I've been OK. Other people have it a whole lot worse. Sure, I experienced a pretty hard three months. I hit a couple low points where I did and said things I wish I could take back. But I can't. So, I have to move forward with the lessons Jesus has taught me through this."

"How do you think humility is different to you now?"

"What do you mean?"

"Matthew, this is the first time since I've known you where you haven't had it all together. You actually seem broken. You often work hard at keeping life together. I know from experience the lessons you're learning now are much different than before. Humility is real now."

"Oh, it's like night and day. I'm only used to temporary humility. And this doesn't seem to be temporary. This is for however long God wants me to be here. And for the first time, I'm OK with that . . . I know I want to learn how to stay here."

"Where?"

"Umm, well, I guess down in the fetal position . . . I want Jesus to hear me say I can't do it on my own. I want to scream it from the mountaintops. I want to put a tattoo on my chest. I *can't do* any of this without his involvement. If I'm not in a humble and uncomfortable position—*like the fetal position*—I will *always* try to do it on my own and not include Jesus in the process . . ."

"Fetal position, huh?"

"I'm not even sure that makes much sense. *Does it?*"

"I get it. Although, I'm not sure I'd tell a whole bunch of people you don't know that you're living life in the fetal position."

"It will be just between you and me *and my mother*—cuz I've already told her."

At Night When I Am All Alone

Sometimes I wake up in the middle of the night with a very full mind.

For some reason our upstairs neighbor is usually still awake at three in the morning. Don't ask me why. I think she must sleep during the day. I usually hear the fifty-five-year-old's footsteps and then the paw-steps of her dog chasing after her down the hallway. My wife and I sometimes lie in our bed and try to guess what our neighbor is doing upstairs. My wife comes up with some hilarious scenarios. But one thing is for sure: we hope she can't hear us as well as we can hear her.

When I'm awake at night, the railroad adjacent to our condo community will predictably have one train that runs by, tooting its horn exactly three-and-a-half times for all to hear. The train sounds so impressive in the middle of the night—it sounds loud and big and fast. But really, it's just loud. At first, when I moved in, the train bothered me, but now it's a sound I associate with home. I'd miss it if it were gone.

When I can't sleep, I do what most Christians probably do—*I pray*. My prayers are a little needy at night. But Jesus understands. He likes it when I'm needy—not codependent, just needy. Once in a while, Jesus talks to me at night. I find it so much simpler to hear him when it's dark and I'm alone. We have a conversation. It's in those moments that I tell him to keep me close by his side. I tell him that I am nothing without him. But of course he knows all of that.

One night when my wife was away visiting her family in Wisconsin, I was awake. It's crazy how quickly after marriage it becomes hard to sleep when your wife isn't in bed with you. So, I lay awake, staring at our white textured ceiling. I just began talking to Jesus. We had a conversation, and yes, I talked out loud.

"What do you want from me, Jesus?" I asked. "What do you really want from me?"

I want you to be a man who is not consumed with fame, wealth, or security. I can use a man like that.

Those were his words back to me. They stung my heart. It's not like I didn't know that; it's just hard to hear it again and then compare it to my life.

"You know how hard that is for me," I replied. *"You know* that kind of life goes against my personality."

You won't ever be that man unless you begin to take on the qualities of my personality, Matthew. You use your personality as a crutch, as a reason not to really follow me. You only dance around with me. But you still haven't truly decided to walk with me.

"You're right; I probably don't."

I keep telling you and reminding you of all the things that truly bless me. But you resist them. You hold back because you like your pride. You like thinking about yourself. You're afraid that following me fully would make you unpopular or make you appear to be a conformist. You know I'm not impressed with the world's opinions. But you are. I see it in your heart.

I stopped talking after that and just quietly confessed. Jesus was right; he's always right. I do hold on to this world so tightly. I didn't think that was a problem with humility, though. I didn't see the connection between how I view the world's perception of me as a *me* problem. But Jesus basically pointed out to me that when I am concerned with what everybody else thinks, I'm putting myself on a pedestal. So again, I stepped down. I have to do that a lot.

Jesus is certainly patient with his kids. But sometimes I've mistaken his patience for contentment. He's not content unless I am moving toward him and then with him. Unless I am craving the humility he desires, he's not very impressed.

Magical kinds of things happen when I'm meek and humble, but only when I'm not forced to be so. When I get on the journey and let go of myself, I begin to see the work of Jesus in my life. That's the moment where being salt and light makes sense. It's in that place where peacemaking becomes natural. Getting humble, putting myself in the "fetal position" before Jesus, makes a heart pure. Humility is a good jumping off point for relearning Jesus, but it's also the core and completion of magic. Humility is the glow which makes all of our good deeds shine.

I've learned that, when I am in a place of humility, I can hear the heart of God. Humility is a place I have to visit often. You don't just suddenly "get there." And when I think I do, it only means I need to go there *again*.

It's a journey.

8

love

Truly loving another means letting go of all expectations. It means full acceptance, even celebration of another's personhood.

Author unknown

When I was six years old, I still loved sitting in my mother's lap. Something was peaceful about leaning back against her chest with my head nestled next to her neck as she gently made the old crackly rocking chair move back and forth. I loved hearing the sound of that old rocking chair; even today, when I hear that distinct noise, I think of my mom. When I was six, I was getting too big to sit there very long. But my mom didn't mind; it was peaceful for her too.

beatitude

While I was sitting in her lap, she'd whisper in my ear, "Do you know how much I love you? Words will never be able to describe how full my heart is for you."

As a kid, I loved hearing my mom whisper. The way her soft voice tickled my eardrum was magical. Not only could I hear her love, but I could feel it too. I never once questioned my mother's love for me. Mom liked letting her family know how she felt about them. Her love was tangible—warm, soft, and inviting. She taught me the importance of wearing my affection on my sleeve. Her love for her family was always intimate and full of touch.

Today, I realize I learned how to love Jesus from my mom. I've watched her over the years learn what it means to fall in love with her Savior. I have always been able to sense when Mom was especially close to Jesus; her time with the Lord always ended up turning into more love for her family. I will never let go of those memories. I want them to stay with me and become a part of my story, become a part of who I am.

I know now that those moments in my mother's lap, when I was probably too big to be there, are the first memories of mine where I *felt* love for somebody other than myself. Something is pure and free about the kind of love a kid feels for their mom and dad. It's the kind of love that's difficult to say out loud—not because you're embarrassed to say it but because you haven't learned the words that even come close to describing it. The love that doesn't need words is magical; it's the kind of love Jesus wants me to show to people—*all people*.

Growing up, I found the concept of "Christian" love bewildering. The "love" I witnessed within the four walls of my church was a form of religiosity that today I wouldn't wish on my worst enemies. The kind of love my church showed could have easily been mistaken at times for abuse, punishment, or carelessness. It was the most unlikable kind of love I have ever encountered.

When you're focusing on enforcing rules instead of embracing Jesus, love is more often than not the first thing to become deformed and tainted. It's hard for love not to get infected when a church is busy managing the actions and morals of people. When the length of my mother's skirt was more important than what was going on inside of her heart, love became sick. When visitors in my youth group would all get ushered into a room and *every one of them* would come out "born again," love smelled. When people would leave my church in anger and no one cared enough to wonder why, love's scent bcame unbearable. That's what happens to love when a church focuses on rules.

My old church often went to the extreme with an intense kind of legalism few are privy to. But I still see glimpses of that kind of thinking and behavior in churches today. It's not so much rules, like hair length and forced salvation experiences, as it is the spiritual expectations put on people. Whether it's speaking in tongues being used as a thermometer for faith, or small group involvement being the end-all-be-all for community, or overprogramming the lives of Christians with seminars, conferences, and studies, the church is still notorious for presenting faith in Jesus as a formula or equation for the content of life. If not careful, the "equation" becomes the focus, and in the process, love begins to smell funny. Sometimes it just plain stinks. I have seen the effects of infected love happen over and over again in the stories of people who have become victims of church gone wrong.

When I hear such stories, my heart aches at the awful way Jesus is being represented to people. Religion can be so cruel. When people are spiritually abused, it's a very deep kind of pain because it hits what often is the core of people—their faith. When a person's faith is infected with poor teaching, abuse, legalism, and the absence of love, the effects are devastating. I know those effects.

But I don't want to mislead. Despite all that I saw in the church, it's not like I didn't *know* love as a kid; the love that held my family together was both a spiritual and relational kind of love. Just as I was able to watch my grandmother be the truth of Jesus in my life, so were my parents and sisters. They were *far* from perfect. But my mom and dad's love for my three sisters and me was the one thing I *never* questioned. I'm convinced it's their love that kept me sane through it all. I watched them *try* to bring a little love and mercy into their church life. They strived to love like they believed Christians were supposed to love, but the rigid nature of legalism always crept in and would overwhelm us. Eventually, we, along with other families in the church, stopped trying.

We left.

Affected by the Effects

As a young adult, I struggled with being a free Jesus-follower because I didn't understand his spiritual command for us to show love. In fact, it goes deeper than even that: I didn't understand God's love. I knew he loved me enough to send his Son to die, but I had a hard time understanding his fatherly love, his love as a friend, his love as someone who would never leave me nor forsake me. As far as I was concerned back then, he hadn't kept up his end of the bargain. I thought he *had* left me. I thought he was mad for conjuring up this ridiculous way of following. I didn't understand the truth back then. Now as an adult, I can look back and see where Jesus didn't forsake me or leave me, but as a kid, as a teenager, as a college student, even in the early parts of my new journey, I was blind to that.

By the time I entered college, I knew more about how to hate sin and sinners than I did about how to show the love of Jesus. And when you have experienced an infected type of love for more than seventeen years, and you've invested a great deal of time into hating sin and those who sin, every aspect of your spiritual life is affected. My understanding (or lack of understanding) of the love of Jesus influenced the way I looked at life, tragedy, friends, dating, evangelizing, romance, missions, church, and service. My inability to love crippled my faith.

Realizing and understanding the truth of Jesus certainly helped. During my time of doubt at Belmont where I got away with Jesus for five months, I most definitely began to experience the love Jesus extends to his kids. But even after all of those beautiful moments with Jesus, breaking the old habits of hate and refocusing my Christian life toward loving people was a strenuous and overwhelming journey.

Unfortunately, I wasn't able to change this kind of behavior overnight. Before I was able to show anything that closely resembled the love of Jesus, it took years of seeing and experiencing how Jesus used the love of Christians in the lives of people. I had to see *how* that love worked in those lives. But after I saw its effects, I then had to accept that work as the love of Jesus and convince my brain not to think of it as a fabrication of his love. I became like Thomas; it wasn't enough for me to hear that Jesus's love existed in a situation, I needed to touch it, stick my fingers through it, and experience it for myself.

Like most of my journey, that was hard. I wish I had a dollar for every time I said the journey was hard. Because often I saw the love of Jesus break some of the rules I once held in high esteem. *Love can't do that!* I thought. *Christians shouldn't be there! Jesus wouldn't be caught dead doing that!*

beatitude

When I watched his love (through people) go into bars, hold a gay man with AIDS, sit down with a prostitute and ignore the weed sitting on the table, and embrace an atheist as a friend, it scared me. It's not that I didn't think it was beautiful. On the contrary, it was the most beautiful sight I had ever seen. But when I saw it, my old way of thinking, my old way of believing would creep to the surface and it would make me doubt the love of Jesus displayed through people would go *that* far.

The process of embracing a life-filled, Jesus-focused love was often extremely complicated. My heart needed to be cleaned. It had to be stripped of all that ailed it and then filled with something new and fresh and clean.

Like a Chicken Coop

I once heard a preacher compare his heart to an unkempt chicken coop. I knew exactly what he was talking about. In fact, I understood his illustration probably better than most—I once raised chickens.

People laugh when they hear I grew up around chickens. "*You* had *chickens*?!" most say, acting as if they'd never met a poultry-savvy individual before. My family didn't have a farm; we owned five acres of land in a rural part of Maryland. My dad has always dreamed about having a hundred-acre farm with cows and corn-fields and chickens. Perhaps as a way of living bits and pieces of his fantasy, but also to teach me hard work and the value of money, my father bought me twelve chickens. (I eventually had slightly more than a hundred.)

I was seven years old at the time, and I raised the chickens, harvested the eggs, cleaned the eggs, and sold them to the nice old ladies at church. I had most of my chickens named and knew their "faces" by heart. And they helped me get to college—in the four years I sold eggs, I raised nearly seven thousand dollars. Of course, my father had probably invested more than that in just feeding those birds. But he didn't care; I learned a lesson and he got a minifarm.

Cleaning out the coop was my least favorite part of having chickens (that, and when the rats would come out at night). Removing the manure was a half-day event for my father and me. With pitchforks and shovels, the two of us would go into my poop-filled chicken coop and clean it out.

The first pitchfork full of dung would release an awful scent in the air. It was sometimes so nauseating to my seven-year-old nose I'd have to run outside for some air and coax myself to go back. That odor of aged chicken manure had a hint of ammonia to it, and after being penetrated with a pitchfork, the aroma would fill that small area quickly. Underneath the manure, I'd find bugs and worms and mice and other things that lived in the excrement of chickens. Just thinking about the bugs and stench makes the hair on the back of my neck feel tingly. My dad and I had to run all of the chickens out of their house, because they loved pecking and scratching around their freshly turned manure. Those chickens would eat almost anything if you let them. Many of them would stand right outside the door, pecking on the door, as if they knew we were doing something incredible inside.

The next nine shovelloads of chicken poop would release the same stench as the first one. But the longer my dad and I worked, the easier the job became and the less offensive it smelled. After every bit of manure was cleaned out and piled high in the back of my father's pickup truck, I'd spread fresh, clean straw all around the chicken coop. I learned to love and appreciate the smell of clean straw. When I'd finally let the chickens back inside their clean home, I'd stand back and watch them. I swear they acted excited about the good smell, the new straw, and a clean slate on which to do their business.

That preacher I heard was right. My heart has been like a manure-ridden chicken coop on many occasions. Throughout my life, I have found my heart on many occasions to be overcome with "crap." The crap is everything from bad theology to pornography to selfishness to poorly chosen relationships—anything that alters the scent of my heart.

By the time my family and I left the church of my youth, my heart had been filled with a lot of junk. Over time, the hate and legalism I experienced turned into bitterness and an unwillingness to forgive. Add a little more time and my heart eventually became full of cynicism, distrust, and doubt. But the one result I remember the most was an inability to love. Eventually Jesus came in with his pitchfork; the stench of his first shovelful was toxic. Of course, when he began to overturn my filth, I wanted to poke around. I wanted to collect a few souvenirs. I wanted to see if I could find anything interesting. He'd run me out. He'd remind me nothing was there for me.

But before I went through the process of surrendering and allowing Jesus to clean out my heart, a lot of people came in contact with a smelly mess.

Meeting the Jerk Inside

"So, do you think this *feeling* between us will last?" I asked my first *true* girlfriend after two months of dating. We had met the first week of my first semester at Belmont.

"*I think* so," she said quietly, as we lay there on her dorm room bed, gazing up at her roommate's bunk bed mattress. It was one of those blue and white striped ones—the kind most college dorms have. I loved looking at the underneath part of her roommate's bed. For some reason, I had always found stripes to be fascinating to look at.

"I've never felt like this before, Laura," I said. That was true. I only managed to get one girl to date me in high school. It lasted exactly four weeks. She broke up with me the day before Valentine's Day. My heart had been broken. I had lost my hand virginity to her when she held it.

"I don't think I've felt this way either," said my girlfriend. She then smiled at me as her memory triggered a thought. "Well, maybe *once*. But that was a *long* time ago."

Laura and I had only kissed at that point. But both of us were certain God had brought us together for a purpose. Surely, our meeting had not been accidental. Neither of us believed in accidents. As the two of us were lying on top of her bedspread, all four of our feet were touching the floor. You were only allowed to be in the opposite sex's dorm room during certain "mixed company" hours. Also, if you were lying on the bed, one foot always had to be touching the floor. I guess they thought nothing "bad" could happen if you had at least one foot touching the floor. Although, some of the people I knew were quite creative.

"Laura," I said. I was having trouble getting my words out. My mouth was dry and felt like it was full of peanut butter. What is it about being nervous and excited that paralyzes the saliva-making organ in your mouth? "I think . . ."

Before I could finish my thought, Laura leaned in and kissed me. Her lips were dry too. It felt like I was kissing something cold and plastic—like I might have imagined kissing a baby doll would feel like. *I have never kissed a baby doll, well, not since I was a kid.* And Laura had a serious case of "dry mouth" breath. I pulled away, trying not to make it too obvious the experience of kissing her right then was not overly pleasant.

"What were you going to say?" she asked, looking deep into my eyes.

I knew what I wanted to say, but at that point, I was thinking: *Can we go back to looking up at the ceiling? It's much easier to breathe that way.*

"Umm, I just wanted you to know that . . ." I kept trying to move my tongue around inside my mouth, trying desperately to create a little spit.

"Do you guys know that I can hear absolutely everything you're saying?" came a voice from the top bunk. "You might want to be quieter." She popped her head over the side of her bed. "Maybe you two could take this obnoxious display of affection into the hallway." Her roommate's voice was loud and unbearable, almost mood-ruining—*almost.*

"Sorry!" Laura and I said in unison.

"You were saying," Laura said, smiling. *Finally*, the words just rolled off my tongue.

"I just want you to know that I think I am falling in love with you."

Laura smiled big.

"Matt, I think I'm falling in love with you too."

Oh, the power of young, stupid love.

Fast-forward this relationship seven months.

"That is Laura calling, I'm sure; let the voice mail get it," I said to my roommate after the phone rang just as I had walked back into my room. Laura and I had just gotten into a huge fight in the middle of a chapel service. Our relationship had pretty much been a bumpy, awful roller-coaster ride since the day we exclaimed our growing love for each other. But somehow we had managed to keep the psychotic escapades of being *Christian* and *dating* going on for many months too long.

Laura *was* calling; she left a message.

"Matt, this is it; it's over. I know that I've said that before, but this time, I mean it. We're through. I am so tired of this whole thing. You are the most inconsiderate human being on the planet . . ."

"Can you believe her?" I said to my roommate as we both listened in while she was leaving the message.

"You're just as bad, Matt," said my roommate, rolling his eyes. "Watching the two of you has been the most entertaining part of my freshman year. I think you both are absolutely insane. It's like watching a poorly edited edition of *Melrose Place.*"

"Well, you heard her; it's over this time."

"Yeah, right. How many times have I heard you guys say that before?"

"I'm going to eat lunch," I said, ignoring his last comment.

"Mind if I go with you?" asked my roommate. "I want to be there just in case Laura shows up. My life always feels a bit better when the two of you are around."

Laura wasn't there when my roommate and I arrived in the cafeteria. So, we got our food and sat down at a table. I was still fuming. I just sat there and complained about Laura as I ate my cold, oversalted green beans. Seven minutes later, in walks Laura.

"Thank you, Jesus," said my roommate. "This is going to be the best part of my day; I just know it."

"Would you shut up? She's probably not going to sit with us, anyway."

"Are you kidding me? You know she will."

We covertly watched Laura walk through the line, walk over to get her drink, and then make the turn toward choosing a table. I could see in her eyes that she had been crying.

"She's walking toward us," I said. "I cannot believe this!"

"*Yes!*" said my roommate.

Laura quietly walked over to our table. She put her tray next to mine. As she got ready to sit down, I could feel the anger boiling inside of me.

"Matt," she said politely. "Can we talk over here?"

"We have nothing to talk about, Laura," I said, looking at her. "This thing between you and me is *over*. You said it yourself in the message. Do we have to keep doing this?"

My roommate watched with delight written all over his face.

"I think I spoke too soon," said Laura.

"*Are you kidding me?* Please tell me you're kidding," I said, raising my voice. "I'm not even sure I *like* you right now."

"You don't mean that."

"Actually, I do, Laura; I think you're a nutcase."

"Please, can we talk about this?"

I got quiet. She kept trying to get me to talk. She kept doing things to show me that she still cared. I was getting madder by the minute. Finally, my anger hit a boiling point, and I said something I regret to this day.

I stood up and slammed my hands against the table as loudly as I could.

"*Laura*, I am so tired of this," I said with as much anger as I could deliver. "Why don't you go *screw with someone* else's life and *leave me alone!*"

I watched as my words created sadness and fear and embarrassment all over her pretty face. Tears began to roll down her cheeks. I left my lunch sitting there at the table and walked out. My display of anger was sadly exhilarating to me.

You would have thought that would have been it, but three days later, Laura and I were kissing again.

Laura's friend Tony caught wind of the argument in the cafeteria, and he had guts enough to confront me. Although I could certainly sense his hatred for me in his eyes, and his words were definitely harsh and determined, his tone was kind—as kind as I could have expected.

He just came up to me one day when he saw me walking across campus. He looked straight into my eyes and told me the way I treated Laura was heartless and not like a man of God "that you supposedly claim to be" would treat a woman. He told me he thought I was disgusting and he didn't know why Laura would waste her time with me. He then closed by telling me to get my life straight.

"I don't know why you think you can treat a person the way you treat Laura, but you need to confess and make things right. Do you really think your actions show the least bit of love? I just want you to know, Matthew; I think you're pretty much disgusting. Laura is a princess; she should be treated like one."

I know that his words were harsh, but he said them very softly. But my reaction to Tony's words was less than appreciative. I was in no place spiritually, mentally, or emotionally to learn anything from this nice guy. To me, at that time, he didn't have a clue about my relationship with Laura. But he was simply caring for somebody he dearly loved as a friend.

I often think about Tony. I would love to tell him he was right—I did need to get things straight. But I haven't seen him in close to a decade.

Years later, after she was married and living happily, Laura and I made contact via e-mail. We both apologized. We both admitted to our mistakes. We don't stay in touch.

beatitude

The only thing I really learned from dating Laura was I knew little about true love. After Laura and I broke up officially, it was another six months before truth and doubt and Jesus finally hit me over my head and made me realize what I had become.

Watching Love

Erin, a girl I met at my first job out of college, knew something about loving people that I didn't know. We met all kinds at the restaurant where we worked together. By that time, I was certainly trying to learn what it meant to love people like Jesus loved them, but I found it often hard and cumbersome. But Erin didn't seem to have too much trouble. Her love for people, no matter where they came from or what they were investing their lives into, seemed to almost seep out of her pores.

Looking back, I believe I learned more about the love of Jesus from Erin than I had learned the twenty years I had been going to church. Investing herself into the lives of hurting and needy people is what Erin did, and once in a while, she'd invite me along for the ride.

"Hey, Matt," said Erin one evening after our shift. "I'm going over to Samuel's house tonight to hang out. Want to come?"

I wanted to go, but it wasn't to hang out with Samuel. I wanted to go only because I had a crush on Erin. From the moment I had first laid eyes on Erin, I had been thinking somewhat dirty thoughts about her. I'm not necessarily proud of that fact, but I'm being honest. I decided to go, despite the fact that Samuel and everything he stood for frightened me out of my mind.

On the drive over to Samuel's, Erin and I chatted about why she hung out with this guy so much. As always, Erin was blunt, but as sweet as Southern iced tea.

"He's a nice guy," said Erin softly. "Why shouldn't I hang out with him, Matthew?"

"I don't see anything wrong with befriending him at work," I said. "He *is* a nice guy. But I just think he's more apt to rub off on you than you are to rub off on him."

"You're beginning to sound like a Christian, Matt," said Erin, still wearing her pretty grin. "Samuel is gay, Matthew; he's not contagious."

"Well, that's not *exactly* true, Erin," I replied. My comment seemed more appropriate inside my head than when I actually opened up my mouth and said it out loud.

Erin's mouth opened wide in shock.

"Matthew Turner!" she said. Then with about as much sarcasm as Erin could muster up, she quipped, "Well, unless I'm planning on having sex with Samuel, which I do believe he might be morally against at this time in his life, I doubt I'll be catching what he has. You're as stupid as you are hilarious."

I felt much more stupid than I did hilarious. But as stupid and immature as I probably came across to her over and over again, Erin never treated me with any less love. I guess she figured I needed as much love as anyone.

When we arrived at Samuel's house, he answered the door wearing nothing but a pair of yellow and green briefs.

"*Oh, my gosh*, guys; come on in," he said. "I just jumped out of the shower. I had no idea what time it was. Let me put on some pants and a shirt."

When he left the room to dress, Erin squeezed my hand and smiled. I just rolled my eyes in embarrassment. "I can't believe he answered the door like that," I whispered into Erin's ear.

"That's Samuel," she said, still grinning.

As Samuel was getting dressed, I looked around his house. It was like a museum. Statues and paintings and small glass figurines covered his living room. I counted three pictures of Jesus on his walls.

"Hey, Samuel," I said, yelling so he could hear me in his bedroom. "Why do you have so many pictures of Jesus hanging on the wall?"

"*Jesus is a hot* —— —— [words too graphic to print in a Christian book]," he said loudly.

When I heard those six words used in one sentence, my jaw dropped.

Erin gave me a look that said *keep your fat mouth shut, Matt.* So, I said nothing. Although, I was pretty certain that our little gathering would be coming to an end shortly. Because I was sure God had turned Samuel into a pillar of salt for talking about Jesus *and* Mary like that. But alas, the mercy of God was proved once again when Samuel's door swung open.

"Sorry, guys," said Samuel, walking into the living room. "Have a seat and make yourselves comfortable."

Erin ran over to Samuel and gave him a big hug. He hugged her back, but picked her up so abruptly the two almost fell over onto the floor. After they had finished doing a *waltz* in the middle of the floor, the *happy couple* sat down next to each other on the largest futon I had ever seen. I walked over to the only seat left in the room; after eyeing it over good, making sure it was clean, I sat down rather uncomfortably.

"Samuel, do you have a candle or incense burning?" I said, smelling the air.

He laughed an obnoxious laugh and then simply said, "No."

"OK. I smelled something sweet in the air; I thought it might be a candle or whatever."

love

Suddenly, after I had finished talking, there was an uncomfortable silence in the room. I could have cut the tension with the fake sword that Samuel had fittingly placed between the legs of a plastic Abraham Lincoln statue.

With Samuel unable to see her, Erin looked at me with a smile and held her hand close to her face and gave me what I thought was the "OK" sign. She obviously knew I wasn't getting her signal, so she made the same gesture three times. But still, I had no idea what she was trying to communicate to me.

"Erin's trying to tell you that I smoked pot before you got here," said Samuel, bluntly. "That's what you smell."

Again, I felt like an idiot. By that time, I was wishing I had gone home to bed and not come out with Erin. Crush or no crush, my gut told me that this embarrassment wasn't worth it.

"So, what in the world are two good Christians doing out here on the *east* side of town?" asked Samuel with a laugh.

The voice inside me had been wondering the same thing.

"Oh, Matthew and I just got out of work, and we wanted to come by and say hello."

"Well, that was nice of you guys."

The conversation that followed, I *mostly* just observed. But it quite possibly could have been the heaviest conversation I had ever witnessed. Samuel wasn't afraid to open up and share. In fact, I learned things about him that I'm *still* embarrassed to say out loud. *And it takes a lot to embarrass me.*

But eventually, the conversation went from sex and drugs and partying to a deeper topic. Samuel displayed his life like it was a new T-shirt he was wearing. He just blurted his story out for two near-strangers to hear. It was almost as if he had been craving a *real* conversation for a very long time.

Samuel told us that only six months before he had been sui-

191

cidal; his then-lover had rushed him to the emergency room after
he had swallowed a few pills. But then he claimed he had done
it all for the sake of drama. "I needed a little excitement in my
life," he said.

He told us about a boyfriend he had lost to AIDS just over a
year before. Then he jokingly said, "I guess, according to you guys,
we'll be able to get together again in hell." But as quickly as the
laughs came, the tears began to roll down Samuel's cheeks when
he admitted he was afraid to die.

I sat there mesmerized by Samuel's words. He kept switching
back and forth between dramatic emotional pain and a sick sense
of humor. Sitting in my chair, hardly able to move, I just watched
Erin.

"Samuel," whispered Erin, "come here. It's going to be OK."

She wrapped her arms around his body. Samuel put his face
against her left shoulder and just cried. Erin was whispering something into his ear, but I couldn't tell what she was saying. After ten
minutes, Erin let go. Samuel wiped his eyes dry.

"I am sorry about this, guys," said Samuel. "I'm sure you didn't
think you would end up spending your evening like this."

"Samuel Potts!" said Erin. "You better not think another thought
about all of this. You know I love you."

Erin patted his knee.

"Hey, Samuel," said Erin with more love than I had witnessed
in a long time, "I don't want to make you feel uncomfortable, but
I was wondering if you might allow Matt and I to pray with you
this evening."

"Please do."

Erin prayed for Samuel that evening. Well, actually, it was morning: 1:12 a.m. We sat there and prayed together for more than
thirty minutes.

In fact, over the next five years, Erin and Samuel remained very close. Samuel continued to live his life, and Erin continued to love him. A couple of years ago I got a phone call from Erin. "I just called to tell you that Samuel has fallen in love with Jesus," she said to me.

"He has?"

"Yep. He called me last week to tell me that he had begun following Jesus a month ago. Isn't that amazing?"

It was amazing, and it left me in disbelief. Though it was five years later, and I was a very different person, I still felt a little embarrassed. But of course, while I believed her story about Samuel to be true, I first had to ask her if "falling in love with Jesus" simply meant he had added another photo of Jesus to his collection.

"Matthew Turner!" she said with a laugh.

"It was just a joke; you know I have to make jokes."

Samuel was simply one of twenty people I witnessed Erin loving. I watched her love a Satanist. I watched her love an addict. I watched her love a drag queen. But perhaps I was most impressed that, despite the fact I was a recovering legalist with a knack for making Jesus comments at the most inappropriate moments, she even loved me. I am convinced I know Jesus more intimately because of Erin.

You're familiar with the old written law, "Love your friend," and its unwritten companion, "Hate your enemy." I'm challenging that. I'm telling you to love your enemies. Let them bring out the best in you, not the worst. When someone gives you a hard time, respond with the energies of prayer, for then you are working out of your true selves, your God-created selves. This is what God does. He gives his best—the sun to warm and the rain to nourish—to everyone, regardless: the good and bad, the nice and nasty.

Matthew 5:43–45 The Message

This Is What My Love Feels Like

I've learned lessons about love throughout my pursuit of Jesus. I believe most Christians do. Life has taught me that becoming a Christian (which, of course, means Christ-like) is, like my faith, not a place where I suddenly arrive; it's more like an expedition. The more artifacts of truth I discover along the way, the more like Jesus I desire to become.

My most extravagant awakening about the love of Jesus came during a very difficult time in life—when I battled depression.

Something was incredibly funny to me about saying "I am depressed" out loud. In fact, when I first looked in the mirror and said those words to myself, it felt like I was delivering a punch line to a somewhat-funny joke. But I laughed. I stood there, looking at myself in the mirror, and I actually laughed. Truthfully, I had felt *depressed* before, but I had never said the words out loud. That would have been unpardonable for me before that day.

Maybe I laughed because depression came *after* Jesus had brought me out of legalism. Because if there were ever a time I should have admitted depression, it would have been years earlier when I was fighting my belief in Jesus. Maybe it was funny because I was considered by many to be spiritually mature and together. That's actually even *funnier* for me to say out loud. Maybe it was because I couldn't *really* pinpoint why I was feeling anxious, codependent, and insecure. Nonetheless, despite the fact that I was content in my relationship with Jesus, I had many of the classic

194

symptoms of depression. And to me, it *was* funny, but the comedy wore off in a day or two.

I've often heard two things happen when you realize you're depressed. You either run directly away from what you believe to be true or you run toward it. For some reason, certainly not any doing of my own strength, I got closer to Jesus during depression. I'm not saying the journey was simple or uncomplicated, because in many ways it was dreadful. But Jesus ran as fast as he could to remind me of what was true. For a year, Jesus and I together climbed the mountain toward sanity. Oh, I definitely tried to lose him a few times, because he liked the steep parts of the mountain, but I had no such luck.

But through the harshness of depression and through the climb Jesus forced me to experience, *finally* I reached a summit of sorts, and it was a flat road where Jesus and I could convene without interruption, without rope, without me being completely exhausted. Once I reached the easy road and got a good look around, I wanted to stay there. I looked at Jesus and begged him to let me set up a tent.

There, on the plateau, I grew spiritually. Some people take advantage of these experiences; I'm certainly prone to, but that time I didn't. I let Jesus teach me. For months I just sat in his lap. I leaned back against his chest and rested as he gently moved the "rocking chair" back and forth. He whispered in my ear, *Do you know how much I love you? You can't imagine the love I feel when I look at you.*

As I sat there, feeling so comfortable, so at peace, so *not* anxious, I was jarred out of the experience when I felt the rocking stop. Jesus's body moved in such a way that something inside of me was startled. I felt his hands move. His legs shifted.

I thought to myself: *I know this feeling.*

When I was six years old and I had been resting in my mom's lap, the phone would ring or dinnertime would come, and my mother would lovingly and carefully move me out of her lap.

Surely, Jesus wasn't doing that.

My heart raced. I was tempted to panic. I must be mistaken; Jesus can't be tired of me just yet.

But sure enough, Jesus wanted me out of his lap. The motions I felt were purposeful and for my benefit. I must admit, I was stunned for a moment—it didn't make much sense. I figured this must have been how the disciples felt when Jesus told them he would be leaving them soon. They wanted to know why. They had questions. They feared. A couple of them were angered and befuddled. Peter even charged he would not let it happen. That's when Jesus looked at him and said, "Get behind me, Satan."

As I felt that experience coming to an end, I got one clear message from Jesus. His words were simple and straightforward: *The healing I give is a part of the journey. Now, take this most recent experience of the fullness of my love and share it—just share it, Matthew—I promise to do the rest.*

While sitting quietly in the middle of my living room floor, two candles were lit on the TV stand, and Bach was softly playing in the background. My face was flat against the black rug that sat in the center of my room. I lay there overwhelmed by the presence of God, dumbfounded by what he had taught me the last few weeks.

The words Jesus had said to me were scrolling over and over inside my brain. I meditated on them. Suddenly and only for a moment, this feeling of ache and frustration and passion and affection consumed me. The sensation both hurt and felt good all at the same time. Jesus just said to my heart, *That's only a small taste of what I feel for the people of this world.* For barely a moment, my spirit got a small glimpse of how deep and intense Jesus loves people. As the weight lifted off of me, I wondered if I could have handled much more.

For several years I had known I was supposed to love people, but there in that moment I understood *why*. It's not because it's the right thing to do. It's not about looking good to the world. It's not so I can feel good about myself. It's not about publicity and fame.

It has nothing to do with me.

I am to love people—all people—because Jesus loves people.

The process is so frustrating at times because, like everything Jesus teaches in Matthew 5, I have wasted so much time trying desperately to make it about me. But ultimately, that's the message he communicates to me again and again—this life I live isn't about me. It's not about my satisfaction, my wealth, my health, my book deal; the message I learned in Matthew 5 is simply this: life is about being a part of his story through loving people the way Jesus loves.

I think Philippians 2 says it much better than me:

> If you've gotten anything at all out of following Christ, if his love has made any difference in your life, if being in a community of the Spirit means anything to you, if you have a heart, if you care—then do me a favor: Agree with each other, love each other, be deep-spirited friends. Don't push your way to the front; don't sweet-talk your way to the top. Put yourself aside, and help others get ahead. Don't be obsessed with getting your own advantage. Forget yourselves long enough to lend a helping hand.
>
> verses 1–4 The Message

An Ending Thought on Love

Love is hard. Even today, Jesus continues to stand inside my often crap-filled heart, and with a pitchfork he cleans up the mess that gets left behind by life. Each time he finishes, he spreads out a new portion of his grace and mercy so I can begin to love again. And I do—I accept the gift and move on. I can't love others without accepting the gift myself.

Jesus says that it's easy to love those who love you back—even those who do not know him do that. "But I say, 'Love your enemies,'" said Jesus. That request has been the hardest of all lessons on this journey. It's hard for me to swallow; it's even harder for me to put into practice. When I think someone has treated me poorly, it's hard to offer love back. Most of the people I have considered enemies in the past have been church people—people who are supposed to be striving to love.

When love finally captured my heart, I had to spiritually observe my life as if I was a spectator. I had to mentally reintroduce myself to all of the people I felt hatred toward, all of those who I had long since forgotten about. One by one, as Jesus brought them into my mind, I realized how much he loved them, and I was to love them too. Some of those people I have been able to make amends with personally. With some I have lost contact. And honestly, a couple people I'm still trying to love. If I were to see them, the pain of life would come back. However, I'm not satisfied feeling like that, because I crave the freedom that comes to those who love. But that comes with learning the Christian life is an expedition, not a destination.

Freedom comes when I love enough to let go of the pain that has turned into the inability to forgive, which has turned into bitterness of the heart, which has often become personal skepticism about the church. The more I love, the more freedom I experience. Because to show love in this world is all about being humble, hungering for truth, showing mercy, pursuing a pure heart, being light, being salt, and being a peacemaker.

I believe it's those ingredients that make love magical for the people of the world to experience and very difficult for some to resist.

9

magic

Why is it that every time I'm with you makes me believe in magic?

Author unknown

The Failure to Master an Unmanageable Domain

Jammin' Java had still not opened for the day. All alone in the coffeehouse, I was standing at the cash register, counting money when the phone rang. It was my mom.

"Matthew," said my mother. As soon as I heard her voice, I could tell that something was wrong.

"What's wrong, Mom? Is Dad OK?" I asked in a panic.

"Your father is fine, Matthew, but I do have bad news."

Mom got quiet for a moment.

"John Peterson committed suicide last night, Matthew."

When my mom told me that news, I remember distinctly saying something back to her, but I can't recall my words. Of course, anytime someone takes their own life, shock and devastation seem like the only response you're able to feel at the time. But as the news of his death wore itself into my heart, I began to ache for John. And I think I ached a little for myself too.

There had been a time when I knew John quite well. But we had lost touch. We had only seen each other a few times since he had been kicked out of my high school in the eleventh grade. Rumors spread quickly as to why he had been kicked out. I'm not sure I ever did learn the complete truth. What I do know is John and I had a very strange relationship in school.

We had known each other since I was four and he was five. On the same exact Sunday, he and I had gone through the motions of asking Jesus into our hearts. From that moment on, the environment where we learned about our Christian faith was exactly the same, but the way we expressed ourselves seemed to be drastically different.

John was the kid who always challenged the rules. He was a free spirit. At times I envied his ability to be free and not care what others thought about him, but more often than not I believed his actions were stupid and pointless. John seemed to be always searching to fill an empty spot in his heart. He was always getting himself into trouble. He was always attracted to the wrong crowd. As hard as he looked for attention and acceptance in high school, he never got what he was looking for. But gosh, he tried.

For weeks he'd try so hard to follow the rules. I can't tell you how many times I watched John go forward to the church altar to ask for forgiveness and to plead with God to guide his steps. Oftentimes, I saw him do this because I was at the altar too. John's prayer seemed to change his life overnight; the next day he would come in acting differently. He'd dress differently. His attitude would be quieter and more focused. Teachers would congratulate him for his good effort. But the change only lasted for a week or two. Sooner or later, he was back in the principal's office, and when that didn't seem to work, the pastor would talk to him. John was just prone to trouble.

Consequently, John made several mistakes that eventually got him kicked out of school. Some of those mistakes followed him like his shadow. Everywhere he went they seemed to chase him. After he left our high school, the few times I saw him he seemed to always be running. And I guess he got tired.

So often, when John's life and death weigh heavily on me, I wonder if he ever found what he was looking for. Did he get a taste of the Jesus I know today? Did he ever have a true experience with mercy? Was he ever overwhelmed by the love of Jesus through the humility and peace of a fellow traveler? *Did he ever see magic?*

My guess is no. John was lost, trying to master the destination of his faith. Instead of journeying with Jesus, I watched him keep going back to the place where he thought his faith existed. He kept looking at that place, hoping that his actions or his works would make it feel comfortable and safe. But when faith is a destination one is trying to manage, it often feels hopeless and impossible.

I sometimes think I know what John felt. When you've never been awakened to the journey of relearning Jesus (or learning Jesus), you just keep going back to what you've been told is true, what you've been told will bring you happiness and joy. John sometimes followed the rules perfectly; he just never seemed to learn that faith was a journey.

If he had, John might have understood it's OK to be imperfect, and he might have experienced the love and mercy of strong arms and the magic that sometimes happens when you walk with Jesus on the journey.

John's life and death continue to be a reminder for me to keep traveling. Whenever I am tempted to stand still and to try to master the domain of my faith, John's story reminds me a faith that settles is not faith at all.

Oh Yeah, Grace

When I sat down on the hard wicker sofa, and he sat down in his comfy leather chair, I felt like I was about to get a psychological exam. Maybe I was. It certainly seemed possible that his eyes, as they gazed at me over his thinly rimmed glasses, might be able to see inside my soul. His concentrated stare made me feel a little awkward. It felt as though I was living a dream I often had that involved a naked me speaking in front of a thousand laughing circus clowns. At the beginning of the chat, I was tempted to try and overcompensate for what he might be thinking about me, especially if indeed he was psychoanalyzing me.

The man I was talking to is a pretty well-known preacher. He's a kind man, but that doesn't make this doctor of theology any less intimidating. His church is moderately large, he's known around his city for his profound understanding of grace, and I have respected his wisdom about faith for many years. Oh, yeah, he doesn't want me to use his name in my book. But ironically, our conversation last year ended up being the jumping-off point for this book. I believe a few of his answers really helped me grasp a fuller understanding of what Matthew 5 is about.

> **Me:** What's the first thing that comes to your mind when you hear someone say "Sermon on the Mount"?
>
> **Unknown Preacher Guy:** A near impossible lifestyle. *I'm*

kidding. Actually, for me the Beatitudes were no doubt the hardest of topics I ever taught about in my church. So, the first thing I think about is all of the work I put into that series.

Me: Anything else?

UPG: And I often think about the Grand Canyon.

Me: *Why?*

UPG: Whenever I read the Beatitudes, I feel like there's a massive gap between what Jesus expects of me and who I actually am. I feel I am on one side of the canyon looking at Jesus on the other side, and I am unable to reach the other side without his assistance. That's what I sometimes see in the beginning verses of Matthew 5—on the other side of the canyon there is this life that I am called to live, but it seems so far away. So, I end up feeling very helpless. Which I think is the point of Jesus's message in Matthew 5—we are helpless without Jesus . . . And I constantly compare myself to Matthew 5. And when I do, I pretty much realize again I suck at being like Jesus.

Me: Do you think Jesus intended for us to compare our lives to Matthew 5?

UPG: Well, I believe when a person rereads Matthew 5, you can't help but run an inventory of your life as you read about Jesus's desires for his followers. But to answer your question: no, I don't think Jesus began his ministry with the greatest sermon ever recorded so we would have more guidelines to follow. Jesus was quite aware that guidelines weren't going to work. I think it's important for us to see that the statements Jesus declared that day on the mountain are not a "new" Ten Commandments . . . But here's the catch: my flesh loves to compare and contrast; it comes naturally for me to look at these statements and try to live up to their depth. In fact, I do it all of the time. *Why?* Because looking at the Sermon on the Mount as a rule book or as a list of expectations is a lot simpler for Christians to understand and to accomplish than it is for us to lean back and depend fully on the grace of God.

Me: But Jesus does care that I live a life of mercy and purity, right?

UPG: Absolutely! But you see, Matthew, we go about it all wrong. Too often we actually try and pursue on our own these "qualities" that Jesus longs to see in us. But we cannot. Jesus is hoping his kids become so compelled by his grace, so mesmerized by his gift of salvation that these principles in Matthew 5 over time become a natural part of one's life who is following Jesus.

Me: But it doesn't come naturally for us, does it? I mean, is a pure heart really normal for human beings?

UPG: You're talking to a Reformed thinker, Matthew. [Laughs.] No, I don't believe a pure heart is something we can strive for on our own. But as Jesus draws us to himself, and as we get to know him, a pure heart becomes more and more possible because of the grace we are experiencing. It's rather simple, really—the more we tie our lives into Jesus and the things he is passionate about, the more *like* Jesus we are able to live. It's not about walking into a situation and saying over and over again, "I want to be humble, I have to be humble, I will be humble." You're only a few notches away from legalism when you try to embrace the teachings of Jesus like that. There's not necessarily a secret or equation to living out the magic of the Beatitudes; a person just needs to desire it.

Me: What's your best advice on pursuing humility?

UPG: Drink daily from the cup of grace, Matthew. I believe wholeheartedly that grace is the key to living this life Jesus speaks so passionately about. Jesus knows we are unable to be humble or peaceful without him. That's why grace is imperative. *But* that doesn't mean Jesus will refrain from kicking us in our butts when we're *not* being merciful or humble. He *often* uses a little "influence" to wake us up to drink from his grace, and as we drink, the easier it becomes to reveal mercy, peace, and humility.

Me: So, you're saying that living this life is more about the journey than it is about trying to get it right?

UPG: Matthew, if you spend your life trying to get it right, you'll fail every single time. But just remember this: the fact that you're asking these questions means you're on that journey. That's the kind of heart Jesus can use. Jesus will open the eyes of those who are engaged in the process of truly wanting to live like him.

Here's to Hitting the Dismount

I've been relearning Jesus for many years now. When I began the journey, I didn't realize "relearning Jesus" meant I would have to relearn how to live my life. But that's exactly what Matthew 5 does in the life of a follower of Jesus. It asks us to live life not on a different level but on a different plane altogether. I am faced with that challenge every time I reread his Sermon on the Mount. With his words, Jesus encourages me to look at my life in the mirror and see the way God sees me. But not only does this chapter reveal that over and over again; I also get a pretty extensive view of the kind of life he desires to see in me.

beatitude

Whenever I get the picture of me in the mirror, through experiences, conversations with people, and even in my own stupidity, I get a view of what God desires. Every time I see it, it makes me wonder again how the people reacted who actually heard Jesus utter those words.

The Jewish men and women who sat listening to Jesus on the mountain must have been overwhelmed by what Jesus showed them in the mirror. In daring them to believe in him, Jesus brought into question their lifestyle. But not only that, the words he spoke challenged more than four thousand years of their ancestral history.

I would think Jesus's points, even those simple to comprehend, like *turn the other cheek* and *love your enemies*, would have left many in the crowd with a few follow-up questions. Matthew's depiction of the event doesn't imply a Q&A session followed the end of his talk. And I'm quite sure he didn't offer sermon notes or sell his talk on DVD at a merchandise table on the top of the hill.

Jesus basically looked at those people, and with a bunch of small messages rolled into one big message, said: "You're about to relearn everything you know to be true about God, because I am here to fulfill every promise he has ever made to you."

Probably to some of them, Jesus was asking too much of them to radically change everything they had ever learned. It's no wonder so many eventually found it hard to have faith and then ended up resisting the whole thing. If I had been there, I probably would have been one of the many who resisted him too.

Although slight, I believe I have an inkling of an idea what the Jewish followers must have felt when Jesus came along and challenged their ideals. Like them, when Jesus asked me to relearn him, it rubbed me the wrong way too. As pathetic as this might seem, the mere thought that I had a flawed view of Christianity would have at one time seemed like blasphemy to me.

Because I was so certain I knew what it meant to follow Jesus, I resisted anything that looked, felt, tasted, or smelled different from what I was taught. Ultimately, Jesus wouldn't let me be. He kept pursuing me to relearn his ways, his ideals, his passions. And when I finally surrendered the first time, I was certain Jesus would be able to make his point in one lesson. However, I *quickly* learned. Some of my *free* friends informed me it would take a lifetime. After thirteen years that has included thousands of times where I have had to surrender to him again and again, I'm *still* in the process of relearning Jesus.

But often surprising to me, I'm OK with the fact I am still in that process. It surprises me because I like the thought of a destination. I like the idea of being able to one day arrive. But that's not the faith we live. As hard as we try to make it that way, it's not.

Even more surprising to me is the fact I don't feel guilty about being OK with the process. In fact, I'm happy about it—not satisfied but happy. Why? Because Jesus doesn't want me to be guilty; he wants me to keep walking with him.

When I consider the lives of Jesus's twelve disciples, I'm pretty convinced they thought the "Christian" life was going to be much simpler than it turned out to be. By the stories they told, they obviously didn't imagine following Jesus was going to mean they were giving up everything that came naturally and normally to them. Even after spending a better part of three years with Jesus in the flesh, they still didn't *really* get his purpose or his teachings.

I know that feeling.

They thought they got it. Most of them seemed quite sure of their faith and reasons for following this God-man. The way they tell the story, it gives the impression they thought that by following Jesus for three years somehow they had *arrived* in their faith.

I know that feeling too.

But when Jesus died, their *arrived* faith got tested. They thought it was over. They believed they were finished with their "little adventure to save the world with Jesus." What they had believed in so strongly was now gone; the place of faith they thought they had arrived at got moved, so they felt lost. And back to their fishing boats they went.

Over the years, I've heard more than a few preachers ridicule the disciples for going back to their fishing boats after Jesus died. They said something like, "Their faith was so small that they just went right back to their old way of living. How stupid can they be? Weren't they listening to Jesus when he said that he was the Messiah? I think I would have been waiting for him somewhere."

I believe the disciples were simply being human. Moreover, I'm quite sure I would have been fishing that day too. The disciples made the same mistake I have made many times—the same mistake that this book chronicles over and over again. They assumed the Christian faith was a destination, and not a journey.

It wasn't until much later when they realized that the kind of faith Jesus desired would probably take them just a little less than a lifetime to fully understand. But they would have never realized that unless they took a chance and lived the life. Jesus wasn't looking for people who were prone to think of themselves as perfect. He didn't need people who would be quick to think they had arrived at an ideal place in their faith. He knows if we think like this, we are putting ourselves in danger of becoming pointless, irrelevant, prideful, and legalistic. The disciples eventually learned that Jesus wanted a few humble people willing to risk their lives, dreams, and popularity on an adventure to save the world.

For years, I believed Jesus wanted me to be perfect. For years, I believed somehow I could find a way to make myself live exactly like he describes in Matthew 5. I thought I was striving toward a destination. I was looking for a place where living out the principles of Jesus would suddenly feel natural to my spirit. But slowly, I have come to know that me becoming like Jesus is indeed a journey. When I finally realized this "relearning Jesus" gig was a journey, something dawned on me. When Jesus asked me to begin this gig thirteen years ago, he never said, "Oh, by the way, you have to be perfect." He also didn't look at me and promise, "If you follow me, you'll eventually know all of the answers to the questions that are running through your mind." And he didn't say, "This life is simple. You'll get it in no time."

You learn lots of these kinds of things on the journey.

The journey has taught me to have the freedom to be honest and admit imperfection; in fact, I'm free enough today to not even try to be perfect. I've learned while traveling with Jesus that I will never have all the answers to some of my big God questions. But I've learned not to let that bother me. In fact, when you can admit not knowing everything there is to know about God, it proves helpful when pursuing humility. I've learned from experience that life on the journey is hard. In fact, it feels impossible at times. For today, when I look back on the road I have traveled on thus far, and I think about the journey I am hoping for in the future, I think I'm OK with it being hard. But truthfully, that sentiment comes and goes with each new encounter.

But still, I learn and relearn.

Through conversations and people, sermons and art, experiences and mistakes, tragedy and complete stupidity, I am indeed in the process of relearning Jesus. All I experience in this life leads me to dig and pursue and wrestle getting to know the things Jesus loves to see come out in my life—peace, salt, light, mercy, truth, purity, humility, and love. It's my sincere prayer that throughout my life I keep learning how to both live and experience the magic these qualities display when they are lived out in the life of a Christian.

Why do I pursue this? Because I long for my faith experience to leave me feeling what I felt when I saw that one-dollar bill suddenly become a twenty: amazed by the magic, left in disbelief when Jesus uses me, and embarrassed every time I miss an opportunity.

Several years after I met Henry Blackaby, I realized something about our meeting. "The magical" I experienced wasn't because Mr. Blackaby's faith had *arrived*. I felt magic because I was talking to a man who, throughout his life, has resisted the urge to stay in one place in his faith. And instead, he was dedicated to a long-haul journey with Jesus, a journey that outwardly expressed a man who was full of joy, contentment, humility, and truth. And the magic I experienced in that large room when Nichole Nordeman presented her new song to a stuffy crowd—that wasn't a sign that Nichole knew something I didn't. I later realized that she was just an imperfect person struggling, just like me, to stay with Jesus on the journey. And the same is true for my experiences with Brian, Lisa, Eileen, Daniel, Darlene Zschech, Erin, and all the others I mentioned in this book whose lives and stories and experiences continue to teach me the truth about living life magically.

Once in a while, not every day, maybe not even once a month or four times a year, but just once in a while, this journey with my Savior gives me a chance to see the magic. But that only happens when I am surrendered to the truth that my life is not about *my* story but about his. Only then do I get to see some of what he taught in Matthew 5 lived out in my humanity.

I continue to resist the urge to stay in one place in my faith. I'm sure that my future conversations, experiences, and stupidity will keep reminding me of that message.

magic

But I never stop looking for God to move through his people. I never get tired of seeing that. Those moments encourage me to continue on my journey. Because all of us need to get a taste of what Jesus meant when he said, "Blessed are . . ."

A magical life is simply one who refuses to stay in one place. A magical life knows that grace will catch him. A magical life is generally not interested in wealth, fame, and power. It pursues making peace, showing mercy, and chasing truth. It's determined to understand what it means to be salt and what it means to be light in this world. It goes after a pure heart with gusto and surrender. It knows humility is the most beautiful of traits. It tries to show love at every turn in the journey, through every pothole in the road, and when exhausted from the elements that surround it.

A magical life is simply one who is on a journey with Jesus. And in the process of that journey will look for an opportunity to make someone else feel as if they've just witnessed a mere man turn a one-dollar bill into a twenty.

Matthew Paul Turner is a social and cultural commentator for today. The author of *The Christian Culture Survival Guide*, *The Coffeehouse Gospel*, and *Provocative Faith*, he has also served as editor-in-chief for *CCM*, the nation's leading Christian entertainment magazine, and music and entertainment editor for Crosswalk.com, the world's largest Christian website. Matthew is also a frequent contributor to *Relevant* magazine. He and his wife, Jessica, live in Nashville, Tennessee. For more information on Matthew or to contact him, please visit www.matthewpaulturner.com.

Jesus wasn't kidding when he said that

"truth
will set you free."

PROVOCATIVE
FAITH

walking away
from
ordinary

Get this book and get
a load of powerful
inspiration for living out
a faith that is passionate,
stimulating, powerful, and
challenging—a faith that
is provocative.

matthew paul turner

foreword by jeremy camp

ℛ Revell
www.revellbooks.com
Available at your local bookstore